E&J

Michael Angelo Williams

Table of Contents

Dedication

This book is dedicated to his deceased father, Mr. Joe Williams.

Acknowledgments

Special thanks to Felita, a loving wife giving support for over 10 years and being that favor from god. Mr. Walter Tut Johnson, a true brother and confidant providing tremendous encouragement and spiritual exhortation to write this book. All praise and supreme thanks to the one and only living God of Abraham, Isaac and Jacob.

About the Author

Michael Angelo Williams was born and raised in the East New York section of Brooklyn. His early schooling at Catholic school St. Peter Clavers in Brooklyn where writing, acting and the importance of prayer was highly significant. He completed the final year of high school South Carolina in June of 1986. He graduated with honors in Writing and awards in speech and drama. Realizing his purpose and God-given talent. In September of 1986, he attended Chowan college in North Carolina for 2 years were he studied Creative Writing, English literature and Biology. He is the father of 5 beautiful children and 5 grand children.

The next 10 years Mr. Williams turned his attention to music and short stories. In 2002, he wrote and produced a music album called 'Fearless', depicting the spiritual side and carnal acts of many African Americans that causes division within a nation of people.

The purpose of his book is to bring truth through fiction. Michael is a strong believer in the Holy Bible, which teaches facts and strong spiritual faith. John chapter 8 verse 32. Ye shall know the truth and the truth shall make you free. E & J strongly shows these attributes. Twin brothers different in skin color and behavior shows a high example of creativity, physical art and holy expressions. Being fortunate to travel and live throughout many communities, he was a member for several organizations helping the young with conscience writing, history and mentoring. In 2011, he helped found H.O.O.D a non profit organization focusing on proper eating habits according to blood type, art illustrating conscience awakening, eulogies for individuals and families experiencing death and music on awareness for children in Atlanta, Ga. and throughout America. In 2016, Michael was hired as a co writer for reality tv actor Damien Matthias's "E-Love," a Multi-Platinum award winning music producer and executive writer for VR Innovator Inc.

He is now the author of his first self-published fictional novel which he hope to change the minds of many readers with truth and spiritual enlightenment.

Chapter One

The curtains caught a warm breeze coming through the kitchen window, swaying in and out as Rebbie stood gazing out into the yard, rubbing her swollen belly. It wouldn't be long before the twins arrived.

She smiled, enjoying the early morning quiet of the house. The only movement and sound came from her moving around the kitchen to make breakfast, singing an old negro spiritual song that had been her favorite since childhood.

> *...wade in the water. God's gonna trouble the water*
>
> *Those children all dressed in red...*
>
> *(God's gonna trouble the water)*
>
> *were the ones that Moses led*
>
> *(God's gonna trouble the water)*
>
> *Wade in the water. Wade in the water children.*
>
> *Wade in the water. God's gonna trouble the water.*
>
> *Those children all dressed in white...*
>
> *(God's gonna trouble the water)*
>
> *must be the ones called an Israelite*
>
> *(God's gonna trouble the water)*
>
> *Wade in the water. Wade in the water children.*
>
> *Wade in the water. God's gonna trouble the water...*

Caught up in the spirit and words of the song, she clapped and then raised her hands. "Yes! My God, my God..."

Just then, one of the babies kicked and her belly shifted. Normally she could feel a lot of movement from both of the babies sharing her womb. But so far this morning, only one of the boys was active.

"Mr. Jones One, you ain't kicking on Mr. Jones Two this morning? What's the problem, baby boy?" she looked down and spoke softly to her unborn child. "You acting strange."

She picked up a spatula and turned her attention back to a skillet on the stove where she was keeping her and Isaiah's breakfast warm. "Oh I know what it is," she said smiling, "you waiting on this turkey and eggs. Too hungry to fight your brother this morning."

Imagining the babies already in a brotherly squabble made her smile even more. "Well, hold on a minute. It'll be ready in just…."

Suddenly, there was a loud sizzle and grease popped from the pan, landing on Rebbie's hand and the front of her nightgown. "Ooh!" She jumped back from the stove, dropping the spatula and protectively covering the front of her body.

Realizing she was okay, she held the edge of the counter and bent her knees to grab the spatula from the floor. But a sharp pain made her stand back up straight. Then another pain, longer and more like a contraction. It was time to call her husband.

"Oh! Oh!" she winced in pain. "Daddy…! *Daddy!*"

Isaiah found Rebbie leaning against the counter, holding her belly with both arms. There was sweat on her forehead and her eyes were wide with pain and fear. He ran to his wife and supported her weight while guiding her to a seat at the kitchen table. He reached for the phone to call their OB doctor.

"Dr. Smith, I think it's time!" he yelled excitedly into the phone. "These pains are coming fast and hard. Just a few minutes apart."

"Okay, Mr. Jones. Bring her on in and I'll meet you there," the doctor said on the other end.

Minutes after arriving at the hospital, Rebbie was in a delivery room in full active labor. Dr. Smith was in position at the foot of the delivery bed, and two nurses stood by ready to assist him. Isaiah held his wife's hand and coached her through the breathing they had practiced over and over in recent weeks. But this wasn't practice - the babies were coming now. He was nervous and happy and scared all at the same time.

"Okay, Mrs. Jones," the doctor said, "you're doing good. On the count of three, I want you to push, okay?" He glanced at Rebbie, and then refocused his attention. "One, two, three, *PUSH!*"

Rebbie bore down and pushed with all her might. "*Hhhhhmmmmm! Aaah! I'm pushing!*" She let out an agonizing scream.

"Hold my hand tight, Baby!" Isaiah leaned next to his wife to encourage her. "You're doing so good!" His lips brushed the beads of sweat on her forehead.

"Ha! Easy for you to say when all you are doing is holding my hand!" Rebbie managed a weak smile. Then, *"Oh...! Oh!"* Her expression changed and she gripped Isaiah's hand even tighter as another contraction started. "Get these boys out of me!"

"Okay, Mrs. Jones," Doctor Smith said. "Just like the last time, I want you to push on three. Ready? Okay…one, two, three, *PUSH!"*

Rebbie gathered all her strength, bracing her feet in the stirrups and squeezing Isaiah's arm on the doctor's command. *"Hhhhmmmm-aaaah!"*

"Good job, Mrs. Jones! I see the top of one head. One more push and we'll have baby number one!" Dr. Smith looked at Isaiah. "Dad, you want to come and see your son being born?"

"Yeah, sure, Doc!" He moved to the end of the bed right behind the doctor, in time to see Baby Boy One come into the world. Dr. Smith held the baby up for Rebbie to see, then handed him to one of the nurses who was standing by. Isaiah's excited smile faded to a look of concern once he saw the baby's face. He looked from the doctor to the nurse, but neither of them seemed to notice anything out of the ordinary. He looked at his wife but realized she had only gotten a quick glimpse of the child.

"Ooh....ahhh mmmm... Oh my god!" Rebbie moaned again from the top of the bed.

"Hold on, Mrs. Jones." Dr. Smith repositioned himself for the next delivery. "Keep up your breathing. We've got one more."

Isaiah leaned behind the doctor's shoulders again. "Hey Doc. What… what's going on?"

"Sorry, Mr. Jones. Can't talk right this second. This other baby is coming now!" He gave Isaiah an impatient look and then turned his attention back to Rebbie.

"Okay, Mrs. Jones. Same as before. On three. One, two, three… *PUSH!*" Isaiah's eyes were fixed to where Baby Boy Two was emerging from Rebbie's womb. He immediately saw the obvious difference between this baby and the first one – this one was Black. *Lord, what have you given me? Black and white twins?* "Doc... what? What's the chance of this happening?"

Dr. Smith swiveled on his stool to face the new father. Isaiah was somewhat relieved to see the doctor did have a look of amazement on his face. It let him know he wasn't wrong. He wasn't imagining things.

"I know what you're asking, Mr. Jones." He held his hands up and shrugged. "What I know for sure is your wife just delivered two healthy, full-term baby boys. Beyond that…" he shrugged again and then stood and walked to the nurses who were examining and measuring the newborns. The room was filled with the cries of both babies.

"What's wrong Isaiah? Honey, talk to me. Is everything okay?" Isaiah realized that Rebbie had been studying their faces and she was now afraid that something was wrong with the babies. She did her best to lift up a little to watch what was being done with them on the other side of the room. "Doctor, are the twins okay? Doctor, can I see my babies?"

"The boys are fine, baby. You did good!" Isaiah softly caressed his wife's hand, trying to put her at ease. A look of relief crossed her face, and she suddenly felt the fatigue from labor and birthing two babies.

"Your husband is right, Mrs. Jones. Everything is fine." Dr. Smith appeared beside the bed. "The nurses are going to finish running some tests – just normal baby stuff," he said with a warm smile. "And we'll have one of them check your vitals, just to be sure everything is fine with you as well."

Soon, a third nurse came into the room and began to check the monitors at Rebbie's bedside. "Alright Mrs. Jones, let's get you checked out." She gently took Rebbie's arm and began to check the monitors again. "Once we finish up and let you get some rest, someone will bring the twins back in. Alright?" Rebbie nodded and studied the kind, steady smile on her face. The very same smile her husband and the doctor had on their faces. Everybody was doing their best to assure her that everything was fine. But something was off. She could feel it.

Isaiah saw Dr. Smith walking toward the door to leave, and without hesitation, turned from Rebbie to follow him out into the hallway. He could finally question him about what he'd seen.

"Okay Doc. Now that she can't hear us…be straight with me. It's not just me, right? I mean, you saw the same thing I did. One black baby and one white," he said, holding out one hand after the other. "Did you... did you know this was coming?"

"Mr. Jones, you saw those two boys being born just like I did," Dr. Smith said in a defensive tone. "No... no! There's no way to know that beforehand." He placed a hand on Isaiah's shoulder, softening his voice and looking him in the eyes. "Besides, they look to be perfectly healthy. Your wife did good. I would just try to relax and enjoy this blessing."

"Right" Isaiah agreed. He took a deep breath and then released a sigh of relief. "Two beautiful and healthy boys. This is a blessing." The two men continued to walk and talk about the events of the morning.

Less than twenty feet away, a group of nurses was gathered together. Two of them were very animated, telling the rest of the group what they had just witnessed. "Girl... you are not going to believe what just happened!" one of Rebbie's delivery nurses glanced over her shoulder like she was about to share some top-secret information.

"What?" another nurse leaned in, rolling her eyes. "Let me guess. Some poor lady just gave birth to a twenty-pound baby." The group all laughed.

"Mm-mm girl, *no!* Not even close." The rest of the group leaned in. "A black couple right down the hall," she looked over her shoulder again and pointed, "Mr. and Mrs. Jones, you know... the people that own Jones Bonding?" She paused for dramatic effect

while most of the women nodded. "Well, they just had twin boys…
one Black and one white!"

There was a collective gasp, and they all looked at the other delivery nurse for her to confirm what the first one had said.

"Yep," the second nurse crossed her arms and nodded, "saw it with my own eyes."

"Oh Mami!" One of the nurses, Charity, traced the sign of the cross over her chest. "Girl! Are you for real?" Another nurse, Felita, had an expression that said she didn't believe the story. "Are you sure? How did that happen?" A trickle of laughter rose from the group.

There was never a dull day in Labor and Delivery, but none of these nurses had ever personally seen or heard of anything like this.

Standing at the edge of the group, local reporter Yvette Norman listened to every detail, already forming a news story in her mind. She covered the healthcare and hospital beat for the city, and most of her stories came from citizen complaints or information she gathered while visiting hospitals and clinics. But this morning, she had stumbled upon something unusual and really newsworthy. This morning she hit the jackpot!

"Ladies?" Dr. Smith and Isaiah approached the group while they were still gossiping. Seeing the doctor, they scattered, each one rushing away in the direction of some patient or duty that needed their attention.

"Well, that's my cue." Yvette quietly followed the two men as they walked farther down the hallway.

"Dr. Smith, let me just say this…" Isaiah continued to plead his case, "I love my God, my wife… and now my two boys. But I just have never seen this before. I need to know, what are the chances of this ever happening? I mean, can *you* explain it?"

"I'm going to be honest with you, Mr. Jones," the doctor said. "I believe the chances are one in a million, maybe less. But again, I know two things for sure," he counted on his fingers, "one… the twins are healthy, and two… I believe you can see for yourself, this may be nothing but God choosing you and your wife to do his will."

Isaiah nodded in agreement. "Yeah Doc, I believe you're probably right. But…" Isaiah rubbed the top of his head with both hands, "it's still just so… so…"

"Look, Mr. Jones, the nurses will be bringing your babies back soon, ready for you to hold. And while your wife is resting, you will get the honor to bond with your boys first. Another blessing in my eyes!" Dr. Smith patted Isaiah's shoulder once more and smiled. "I tell you, I will never forget this experience."

"Thank you, Doc. For everything. God bless you." "God bless you and your wife. *And* your new family! Take care, Mr. Jones." They parted ways, walking in opposite directions as Isaiah made his way back to Rebbie's room.

Taking advantage of the moment, Yvette approached the doctor. "Excuse me. Dr. Smith?" He turned to face her. "I'm Yvette Norman with WBTZ news."

"What can I do for you?" He gave her a tense smile, realizing she must have already heard the news of the day.

"Well, I'd like to ask you some questions about what just happened. Dr. Smith, is it true?"

"Is what true, Miss Norman?" "Is it true that an African American woman gave birth to twin boys this morning… one black and the other white?"

"Yes. That is true." He noticed the reporter's satisfied expression. "But before you ask, no, they will not be giving any interviews today. Please respect their privacy and allow them time to enjoy their newborns."

Chapter Two

"Congratulations, Mr. Jones! Here's your strong, beautiful wife." A nurse greeted Isaiah when he re-entered Rebbie's room.

"Thank you!" He nodded and smiled. He could see that Rebbie was awake, propped up in bed, still looking drowsy and tired. Seeing him, she perked up a little.

"Hey, Daddy," she said, reaching for him. "How are the babies?"

"Everything's good, Baby. The boys are fine."

"I'm a *big girl*. I finally did it!" she flashed a wide smile.

"Ain't no denying that. This is no make-believe."

"You're right about that, Daddy."

The door swung open, and a nurse peeked inside. "Mrs. Jones, if you feel rested and the two of you are ready, I'll go and get the boys and bring them to you."

"Okay. That'll be fine, thank you," Isaiah answered and watched as the nurse left the room.

"Isaiah, help me sit up in this bed so I can hold our boys when they bring 'em in." Rebbie tried to scoot back to rest against the pillows. "How do they look? Are they identical?"

"They look fine, Baby." He smiled and moved closer to help her sit up, but she could see there was still something behind his smile. "Um… look Baby, let me read you a scripture before they bring the boys in." Isaiah found a copy of the Holy Bible in one of the drawers beside Rebbie's bed.

"Okay." She felt something had to be serious. "Hand my shawl over here so I can cover my head." Isaiah read aloud from the 25th chapter of Genesis. When he was done, he slowly closed the book and stared at his wife, waiting for her reaction. "Isaiah Jones," she said with a look of awe and confusion, "are you saying that I gave birth to a Black *and* a white baby?!"

"Looks that way." He placed the Bible back into the bedside cabinet.

"But…" Rebbie looked bewildered.

"That's just what it is, Baby. So we got to be strong." Isaiah squeezed her fingers and then stroked her cheek.

"Isaiah, are you sure? One of them is *white*?" She searched his face to see if there was any doubt in what he was saying.

"Woman, I know what a white baby looks like! *Yes*…yes one of 'em is white." He managed a small laugh, hoping he had not startled Rebbie or hurt her feelings. What she said next actually helped to calm him down and bring his attention back to the important thing, which was the babies.

"The father controls everything."

He looked at her lovingly, proud of how calm she was. "Absolutely," he agreed.

"Are they healthy?" she asked with a mother's concern.

"Yes, both healthy. Five pounds three ounces, and five pounds eight ounces."

Rebbie beamed with a contented smile. "Which one was the eight ounces?"

"Jacob," Isaiah answered. "Jacob is five pounds eight ounces."

"Oh! You named 'em already? So I guess the other one's named Esau?"

"Well… no, I'm not saying that Baby, but…"

"Wow! Yeah Isaiah, how about E and J?" Rebbie looked at her husband, hoping for his approval. "Our white son, we can call him E. And his brother J. Who came out first?"

"Um… that would be E. Five pounds three ounces."

"You okay with their names?"

"That's perfectly fine, Baby. I don't have a problem with it. In fact, I love it!" Isaiah leaned over his wife. "Give me a kiss."

They heard a soft knock on the door, and then watched the two delivery nurses enter, each pushing a bassinet that carried a tiny bundle wrapped in a fuzzy blue and white blanket. "Hello," one of the nurses chimed in a sing-song voice, "your boys are here!"

"Oh!" Rebbie sat up straight again and held out both arms. "Bring my sons to me!" The nurses handed a baby to each parent, E to Rebbie and J to Isaiah. Rebbie gently adjusted the blanket and stared into the face of the tiny human she held in her arms. She was visibly overcome with emotion. "Isaiah look! Our sons are so handsome!"

"Yes, they are!" He beamed with pride, slowly rocking and staring into the face of the tiny bundle in his own arms. "Very handsome boys."

"Let me see Baby J." Rebbie turned her attention to her other son. Isaiah leaned down so that E and J were side by side.

"Oh, what a nice picture," one of the nurses said.

"Thank you!" Isaiah said. "Do you mind taking a picture of us with the babies?"

"Of course not. What an honor!" she said. "I get to take the very first picture. Unforgettable!" She took their camera and focused on the young family in front of her. "Ok, cheese on three. One… two… three…" she joined Rebbie and Isaiah in saying "*Cheese!*"

"Now that's a beautiful picture," the other nurse said.

Another soft knock broke the moment, and everyone looked toward the door. Soon a smiling face was peeking into the room. "Is this the Jones room?" It was Rebbie's best friend, Leah.

"Yes, it is," one of the nurses answered, moving to allow Leah through the door.

"What's up girl! Come on in!" Isaiah used a free hand to motion Leah into the room. A huge bunch of balloons trailed behind her as she rushed in excitedly. Isaiah laid J gently in Rebbie's arms next to his brother, then reached to grab Leah in a tight hug.

"Hey, big brother! Finally got that Daddy title, huh?"

"Don't you know it! Can't tell me *nothin'*. I did my thing!" Isaiah puffed out his chest with a sly smile on his face.

"Mm-hmm…. alright *Mister I did my thing*!" Everybody in the room laughed. "Anyway, Auntie is here! Where's my babies at? Auntie nephews…"

"Hey, Auntie Leah!" Rebbie said. "Come see these beautiful boys!"

Leah left Isaiah's side and walked toward Rebbie and the twins. "How you feel, Mommy? After pushing out them big linebackers?"

"Girl…" They both laughed.

Just a few steps from the bed, Leah stopped in her tracks. Her hands went to her chest and she stared at the newborns. "What the…?" She looked at Rebbie in disbelief. "Is everything alright? Big Sis, you are holding a white baby in one arm and a black one in the other one, right? Are these my nephews, *the twins*?" She spun around to face Isaiah. "Somebody switched babies on y'all! Isaiah! You need to call Joe and find out who did this. They need to be hunted down!"

"No, no calm down Leah! It's not a mistake," Rebbie said calmly.

"What? But…"

"These are *both* our babies. God gave us two healthy boys. Trust me," Rebbie said, "it was a shock for us, too. But everything is fine." She looked lovingly from one sleeping infant to the other.

Leah turned back to Isaiah to see him nodding in agreement. "Well," she shrugged, "if the father did it then I got no reason to complain. But I *do* know one thing… Black *and* white people are going to bug out when they see this!"

"Girl, you ain't telling no lie!" Rebbie said, and they both laughed.

"Okay, so enough now. Let me hold one of my nephews." Leah reached down and lifted J into her arms. "Oh my, so handsome! What are their names?"

"That's Big Boy J you got right there," Isaiah said proudly.

"J? What is the J for?" "Oh that's another story," Isaiah said. He and Rebbie looked at each other and smiled.

"He has a head full of hair, Isaiah. And your eyes." Leah nodded toward Rebbie and the other baby boy. "What's his brother's name?"

"E," Rebbie answered.

"Girl, don't make me drop this baby!" They all laughed. "Nah, Auntie just kidding," Leah said, kissing the baby gently on the forehead. "So, it's a J and E thing?"

"No, more like an E and J thing," Isaiah corrected her.

"What? Isaiah stop playing." Leah looked to Rebbie. "Sis, for real, what's these boys' names?" "He's serious Leah. E and J."

"But… That's brandy liquor! You mean to tell me y'all named these boys after some brown liquor?!"

"Like I told you Leah, it's a long story," Isaiah explained. "Something you can't handle right now. Trust me."

"Leah, you need to stop being silly! I'm still in recovery and you're making me laugh!" Rebbie winced in pain.

"Ooh, sorry Sis," Leah apologized. "Well, I don't care what your names are." She looked from J in her arms over to his brother E. "Auntie Leah got love for y'all anyway." Then her nose twisted, and she held the baby close and took a deep breath. "Uh-oh… Somebody just did a number two. Isaiah!" She held J out towards his father. "Got a job for you."

"Already?" He looked bewildered.

"You got first shot, Honey," Rebbie said. "And don't put the pamper on wrong!"

"Oh, y'all got jokes! Watch me do it right. Come on Big Boy J."

Once Isaiah had J, Leah turned to Rebbie and scooped the other baby up into her arms. "Here we go," she cooed. "Come on Mr. E, Auntie's handsome *white* nephew." She cut her eyes mischievously at Rebbie and giggled. "All red in the face, with your cute self!" The baby opened his eyes and seemed to respond to Leah's voice as she twirled slowly and kept speaking softly to him. "You and your brother better have love for each other, too. Oh, and watch out for them girls. *That's right*," she cooed in a sing-song voice. Then she looked at Rebbie. "I gotta speak the truth. I was a little scared when I drove up."

"Why? What scared you?"

"When I drove up, two news trucks were parked in front of Emergency. *Now* I know why!" she rolled her eyes and laughed. "You and Isaiah making these designer babies!"

"Girl, you crazy! Designer babies?" Rebbie braced her stomach, trying to stifle her laugh because of her sore belly.

"Yep, *designer babies*."

Another knock at the door stopped their laughter. Holding J securely in one arm, Isaiah went to the door to see who it was. The woman standing on the other side wearing a gray pantsuit looked vaguely familiar. But he couldn't figure out where he'd seen her face. "Can I help you?" he asked.

"Hello, sir! Are you Mr. Jones?"

Isaiah frowned suspiciously. "And… who are you?"

"Oh! I'm sorry" she said, stepping forward slightly. "I'm Yvette Norman with WBTZ. Are you Isaiah Jones, owner of Jones Bail Bonds?"

"Sure am! Somebody needs a bail bondsman?" He smiled, loosening up a little. It still hadn't dawned on him why she was there.

"No no no! I'm sorry. I'm here about the babies." She watched Isaiah's expression change and let out a nervous little laugh. She saw him move square into the middle of the doorway in a protective stance, but took a deep breath and continued. "Sir, did you and your wife just have twin boys? One Black and one white?"

The nerve of this woman, he thought. "Yes, actually we did. But my wife is resting, and we won't be giving any interviews."

"I completely understand and respect that, Mr. Jones. But this is truly an amazing story!" She handed him a small white card printed with her name, phone number, and the name of the news station. "In a day or two, I hope you will consider granting me an interview. Maybe at your residence?" She raised her eyebrows hopefully.

"Miss Norman, me and my family know the media hype this is gonna draw," he glanced over his shoulder and continued with a lowered voice, "so we will wait for instructions."

"Instructions? What instructions?" The reporter looked puzzled. "Instructions from who, Mr. Jones?"

"Have a good day, Ms. Norman. Goodbye." Isaiah began to close the door.

"Just one more question, Mr. Jones! What are the babies' names?"

"Thank you, Ms. Norman. Nothing else to say right now. I got your number."

The reporter tried to get a quick glance around Isaiah to see into the hospital room. "Call me, Mr. Jones!" she shouted just as he closed the door.

Days later, Isaiah and Rebbie were driving down their street bringing the twins home and were surprised to see a group of unfamiliar vehicles and what looked like reporters camped across the street from their house. "What the…" Rebbie murmured, staring at the people outside her window.

"Told you, Baby," Isaiah said. "That's why I called Joe." Pulling into their driveway, Isaiah recognized Yvette Norman as one of the reporters. She and a cameraman started to cross the street, heading toward the car. But they were stopped in their tracks.

"Excuse me, Miss!" Joe barked in an authoritative tone. "You gotta back it up! No cameras on the property. Keep your equipment across the street."

"No… I don't think you understand, sir," Yvette argued. "I already spoke to Mr. Jones and he…"

"No, *you* don't understand!" Joe pointed back across the street. "As long as you stay over there, we won't have a problem."

"Larry, get the shot!" Yvette yelled to her cameraman right as the Jones's drove past. He managed to slip past Joe and focus for a clear view of the family inside their vehicle. Joe turned and collared the guy and pulled him back, away from Isaiah and Rebbie's yard. He couldn't hear Rebbie cheering from inside the car.

"There you go, Joe! That's right, tell 'em! Push 'em back! Won't be no pictures today!" She bounced and punched the air with her fists. "Uuuugh! These people don't respect nobody's privacy!"

Isaiah watched her sink back against the seat, losing her energy for a second, and then taking long deep breaths."Relax, Baby! I'm 'bout to put a stop to this right now. I'm not having it." They pulled into the garage and as soon as he turned off the ignition, Isaiah was out of the car headed toward the scene in the street. "Sit tight for a minute while I go and get some things straight!" He walked to Joe, who was standing alone at the top of the driveway. Reporters were yelling to him from across the street.

"Mr. Jones! Mr. Jones! When can we get a picture of the twins?" And, "What are their names, Mr. Jones?" And finally, "How does it feel to have fathered a white baby?" Isaiah heard a flurry of clicks, and the glare from sunlight hitting camera lenses caused him to shade his eyes.

"Hey, Joe!" The two men clasped hands and then embraced in a brotherly hug.

"Congratulations, man!" Joe gave Isaiah a firm pat on the back.

"Thanks, man. Appreciate it."

"No doubt, no doubt. But for real man... what is all of this?" Joe turned around, waving his arm at the reporters and cameras lining the other side of the street. "What are they talking about? All of this because y'all had twins? Can't be."

"Nah, man. It's something more than that," Isaiah confessed.

"I just heard one of 'em ask you how it feels to be the father of a white baby. What does *that* mean? Is there something I need to hear from you?" Joe looked at Isaiah, searching his face for answers.

Trying to change the subject, Isaiah smirked and pointed across the street toward Yvette and her cameraman. "I see you had to back up that lady reporter right there. Miss Norman."

"Oh, you *know* her?" Joe asked, sounding surprised.

"Yeah, she came to the hospital right after the twins were born, and we spoke briefly. She does her job *too* damn well."

"Well, here she comes again." Joe noticed the reporter heading across the street again and stepped between her and Isaiah.

"It's alright, Joe. I got it. I can handle this one."

"You sure? I mean, I can probably shut it down and get her to leave for good."

"No, thanks bruh. I got it. Matter of fact, you go on over and check out what's inside the car!" Isaiah smiled and patted Joe on the shoulder, then turned to face the reporter. "Miss Norman! If you and your people are not out of here in five minutes, you can forget that interview you asked for."

Joe approached the car and opened the front passenger door to give Rebbie a tight hug. "Hey, sis! The father done gave y'all that blessing."

"Yes, he has!" Rebbie smiled brightly. "We got them boys in the back. Go on and take a look."

"Yeah, I got to, 'cause them reporters over there screaming 'bout some *white* baby." Joe opened the door behind Rebbie and was taken by surprise. "*Whoa!* Oh shit! Rebbie you got a white baby in your car!"

"I know that Joe," she laughed. "That's one of the twins."

"Oh… for real?" He was back beside Rebbie, looking dumbfounded and scratching his head. "So… his brother is white too or black?"

"They're both right there, Joe! Go ahead and take a look."

"Oh wow! He's black! How did *that* happen?"

"Who do you think did it?" Rebbie turned in her seat.

"Isaiah didn't. That's God! He got his hand all over that." Joe gave Rebbie a somber look.

She pointed to one baby and then the other and said, "That's E and that's J."

"Word? That's what it is then. I'm feeling those names."

Chapter Three

Six months passed, and Isaiah and Rebbie found themselves sitting side by side in two very uncomfortable chairs, holding the boys and waiting for Yvette Norman to ask her next question. After talking it over with Rebbie, Isaiah used the number on Ms. Norman's card to call and let her know she would be granted one interview. Rebbie had refused to allow Yvette or any other newsperson inside their home, so they agreed to bring the babies to the television station and answer questions for an exclusive story.

"So I assume, Mr. Jones, that you were in the delivery room at the time your wife was giving birth to the twins?"

"Witnessed everything from start to finish," Isaiah answered. He put his arm around Rebbie and gave her a squeeze.

"Can you tell me what was going through your mind at the time? Seeing something that you truly were not expecting."

"It really *is* something that you can't prepare for. Something you don't expect to happen. So, when you receive such special creations that only he... my God can create," Isaiah pointed a finger and lifted his eyes toward the ceiling, "you must examine all things and consider the importance of what was given."

"I see," Yvette said, gave the couple a lingering stare. "I can just *feel* the strong bond between you. An entrenched spirituality that many other families can learn from."

About five minutes into the interview, Rebbie started to feel more comfortable. She was glad they were being given a chance to actually tell their own story. She told Yvette, "We receive a test every day, which produces lessons for us to learn from. You hear *What did you say when you saw this?* Or *What did you do?*" She leaned toward Yvette. "How will you handle yourself if the unexpected happens? All to test your level of common sense on a daily basis."

Isaiah chimed in, supporting his wife, "Our boys will give us lessons to learn from, so when questions pop up and answers have to be given, we will be used as a vessel to teach our sons and society. We understand that some folks may look and say negative things concerning our sons being different colors. So giving them truth, discipline, and love to help establish stability in their lives is mandatory."

"Amen," Rebbie said softly and nodded as her husband continued.

"Even looking forward to their first day of school. knowing what some students may say about J's color, and how that might upset E. Some children may not even know they're twin brothers. So, this is why unity and loyalty is what we pray for."

"So again, lessons must be learned?" Yvette asked.

"For sure! This is not about me or my wife, or even the boys. It's about the will of God. We are his children, so doing the right thing is so beneficial."

"Wow! You two are so made for each other." Yvette smiled at the couple, noting that they truly presented a united front.

"Thank you so much." Rebbie bounced one of the babies on her lap. "Tell her thank you, J!"

"So this is J, and that's E?" Yvette asked, nodding toward the infants.

"Yes, something easy to remember," Rebbie said as she and Isaiah shared a smile. "You are so right, Mrs. Jones. Oh my! I can't get over them... How *adorable!*" Yvette leaned forward smiling, trying to get a giggle out of one or both of them. They were adorable, but she knew instinctively to keep at a certain distance.

"Thank you," Rebbie said proudly.

"So," Ms. Norman began wrapping up the interview, "once again, on behalf of myself and everyone here at news station WBTZ, thank you for this spectacular interview! You've shown us what family should be about. We wish you the best of luck."

"Thank you," Isaiah and Rebbie answered together.

*****

Rebbie had spent all morning trying to contain the boys' excitement once they found out she was taking them to register for school. Most of the time it was almost impossible to get them both dressed and ready to leave the house, especially if Isaiah wasn't there to help. But *this* morning they were perfectly happy to sit side by side, keeping still while she put their clothes on, washed their faces, and brushed their hair. Now, they were skipping ahead of

26

her across the brightly lit lobby inside the local elementary school. She found a doorway marked Front Office and called to the boys to follow her inside. There was a woman behind the counter, busy working at a desk that was stacked with different color folders. "Hello, may I help you?" she smiled and greeted Rebbie and the boys as they came in.

"Yes. I'm Mrs. Jones, and I'm here to enroll my boys for school."

The woman pointed at J and said, "Okay, we can start with him first. The other child will need to have a parent or legal guardian come in to enroll him."

"Wait a minute!" Rebbie laughed. "You think I'm his babysitter, don't you? Well, I'm not. Both these boys are my sons. This is E, and this is his brother, J." She raised her eyebrows, looking directly at the woman behind the desk. "And your name is?"

"Please forgive me, ma'am! I am so sorry!" The woman stood and walked from her desk to the front counter. "I'm Ms. Long." She looked at Rebbie and then at each of the boys. "I had no idea you were his mother," she said nodding toward E.

"I sure am. Maybe next time you should ask before assuming things."

"You are so right, ma'am… um, I mean Mrs. Jones. Again, I am so sorry. I have the forms right here." She reached for a stack of papers at one side of the counter and slid them toward Rebbie.

"I just need to see original copies of their birth certificates and shot records."

"No problem. I have everything right here." Rebbie pulled the documents from her purse and placed them on the counter. She actually felt a little sorry for the poor woman, whose face was turning colors as red crept up from the collar of her blouse.

"Hi, boys!" Ms. Long smiled and waved to the brothers.

"Y'all tell Ms. Long hello," Rebbie said without looking up from the sheet of paper in front of her.

"Hey Miss Long," J said and waved shyly. E waved, but did not speak.

Another woman walked into the office with a little boy, and Rebbie slid her purse and the paperwork over to make room on the counter. The boy looked at E and J who were standing to one side holding each other's hand. "You coming to this school?" the boy asked the twins.

"Yeah," E told him, "Why?"

"Why are you holding that black boy hand?"

"He's my brother," E said. "We twins."

"Y'all ain't no twins! You lying!"

"Darius!" The boy's mother looked away from her conversation with Ms. Long and scolded him, "Don't be calling him a liar!"

"But Mama, he said they are twins," he argued, pointing in E and Js' direction.

Darius' mother looked at the twins and was immediately puzzled. "Twins?" she muttered to herself. Rebbie listened to it all and continued filling out her forms with a smile on her face. Another woman walked into the office leading a young girl by the hand. The girl looked happily at the other children.

"Hola!" She waved at the three boys. "My name is Angela."

"Hey! Hola!" Darius piped up immediately. "You going to this school?"

*****

"Yo, take a look at this." Joe reached over to hand Kenya a suspect's file. Their desks faced each other in the small office.

"What's up?" She opened the folder to scan the first sheet of paper.

"Got this female pimp. Tonya Day, aka Big Suga. She's wanted for assault with a deadly weapon on a minor. Out on a twenty-thousand bond. I got some good info."

"Oh yeah? What'cha got?" Kenya was suddenly very interested.

"She pushing a pink Cadillac from South Carolina to South Georgia, running young girls in Dublin County at a strip spot. Dancing and performing sex acts."

Kenya closed the folder and slapped it down onto the desk. "Suga the Witch like destroying young girls. I gotta put the cuffs on her quick. I hate that kind of evil, JoJo."

"I feel you. Once we handle our business here, we can leave and get there by four or four-thirty at the latest. I got the address." Joe picked up a small piece of paper from his desk. "Small town, so we might get lucky. A pink Cadillac is something easy to spot."

"Yeah, think she's the Pink Panther!" Kenya threw her head back and laughed.

"I'm telling you, she doesn't hold back," Joe told his partner.

"JoJo, you know I don't mix business and personal. But my fourteen-year-old niece was pimped by her mama. So this runs deep for me." Her expression was dead serious. "But don't worry, I'm cool."

"Mmhmm... alright." Joe eyed his partner, hoping she really was cool about everything. "Ok, so let's go on down there and get this bitch." He gave Kenya another long, serious look. "But don't kill her, okay?"

She shot him a wicked grin. "Might rough her up a little JoJo, that's all."

"And *why are you* stuck on JoJo? My name is Joe!"

"JoJo sounds *cuter*!

*****

Isaiah sat on the living room sofa watching a western on tv. E was beside him, twirling a toy in his fingers and trying to imitate the tricks the cowboys were showing off on the screen. Isaiah noticed that E got quiet and turned to see the boy staring at him.

"Pop?"

"Yeah," Isaiah answered.

"We were at school with Mama and a boy asked me why I was holding J's hand."

"And what answer did you give him?"

"I said 'cause he is my brother. My twin brother. But Pop, he said I was lying!"

"Listen, son. A lot of people won't believe you. But the truth is what matters, right?" E nodded and seemed satisfied with his Dad's answer. Isaiah turned back to his program.

"Pop, can you buy me a F-41b9 water gun?"

"A what?!" Isaiah looked at his son and couldn't help but laugh. "E, did you even hear what I just said?"

"Yessir."

"Boy…" Isaiah shook his head and laughed again. "No… well not now anyway. You gotta show me and your mother good grades and good behavior in school first. Plus, I bought you two water guns already this summer."

"I know, Pop. But this one shoots farther. And guess what?"

"What?"

"It's got a scope like the one you got on your hunting rifle!"

"No, E. Now that's where you went wrong. Pop's got the real deal. Dad don't play with toy guns no more." Isaiah grabbed the tv remote and turned down the volume. "You and your brother play with toys. But when you become a man you must put them away."

"No more *toy* guns, right?"

"Exactly, son. You have to be a leader and take on responsibility. So, the first day of school is when it starts for you."

"Okay, Pop. I'll be ready." E's serious expression let Isaiah know his words were sinking in. He rubbed his son's head and then turned the tv volume back up so they could finish watching the movie.

That evening, J sat at the table drawing while Rebbie moved around the kitchen, tidying up after dinner.

"Look, Mama!" He proudly held up his finished picture.

"You got to hold it up higher, Baby. Mama's hands are full right now." Rebbie looked over to where J was holding the piece of paper above his head. "Ooh… I like that! That's a pretty building. Look like you and E's school."

"It is, Mama. That's my school, and I'm drawing it for you!"

Rebbie stopped her cleaning and smiled at her son. "You like drawing, and that's a good thing."

"What's so good about it?"

"A blessing, Baby. You might have been an artist when you were on this earth before."

J gave her a puzzled look. "Huh? I was here before?"

"Listen, J. There's nothing new under God's sun."

"Nothing?" His expression showed deep thought on what his mother was saying.

"Nothing, Baby. Everything is reincarnated. Same spirit, just another body."

Chapter Four

Big Suga bopped her head to a song playing in the car as she drove toward the club. The music was loud, but was still drowned out by the chatter between the other three women in the vehicle, all dancers. Shy, Luscious, and Wet Dream. Shy turned and looked at the two in the back seat. "I'm telling y'all bitches, we gotta get this paper tonight! You feel me?"

"Hell yeah!" Wet Dream agreed. "I'm feeling that!"

Luscious chimed in, moving her head to the beat of the music. "That's right! Time to turn it out and empty them pockets! Time to give up that loot!"

"Y'all better! This ain't no vacation." Big Suga turned down the volume of the music. "Tonight, I want *both* floors poppin! Them solo hos, I got them. Y'all just keep ya asses in them laps."

"*Heeey!* Make that booty clap!" Luscious raised her arms, grinding to the music.

Wet Dream looked at her and laughed. "Luscious, yo big booty need two laps at one time! I done told you, girl... Start bouncing that big ass on two niggas at a time." They all laughed.

"Might as well." Big Suga looked at Luscious in the rear-view mirror. "Big ass booty fucking up my shocks!"

"*Shiiid...* y'all crazy!" Luscious fell against the door laughing.

"Uh-uh, hell naw, we ain't crazy. Add that shit, feel me? Dazzle them niggas from the jump. Old retired Navy captains, young dope boys..." Big Suga was getting amped behind the wheel. "Empty them niggas' pockets! That's what it is, right?"

"You know I will! Anything for that paper!" Luscious said.

"Damn right!" Big Suga said. "Dance for two muthafuckers at a time. Get paid faster!"

"Yes, honey! I'm coming' out there with some fishnet stockings all over this ass." Luscious ran her fingers up and down her hips and thighs. "Y'all hos just don't be hatin'!"

"Alright then, bitch." Big Suga slowed and turned the car into a drug store parking lot. "Go on in there and get some fishnets for that big booty!"

Wet Dream tapped Big Suga on the shoulder. "That's Lil Kim... turn that shit up!" She bounced to the beat of the song. "I'm the baddest bitch! I got that ill na-na! Eat my pussy while I watch cartoons!" Big Suga turned the music up to a booming level as Wet Dream kept rapping the lyrics of the song. They were all caught up in the vibe, enjoying the night and looking forward to taking care of business. Wet Dream and Shy opened their doors to get out and go into the store. Nobody noticed the silver sedan coming off the interstate ramp and slowing down as it passed them.

"Well, look at that," Joe said in disbelief. "You couldn't ask for a better blessing."

"What?" Kenya sat forward and looked from one side of the street to the other.

"Over to my left, in the CVS parking lot," Joe said and pointed. "Ain't that a pink Cadillac?"

"Well, I'll be damned. Sure is!" Kenya slapped the dashboard. "Your eyes ain't deceiving you. Let's do it!"

Joe drove on a little farther, then made a u-turn. "Let's hope Big Suga is driving."

"How sweet is this?" Kenya quipped. "Miss Tonya Day buying her girls a little treat."

Inside the store, Wet Dream and Shy stood in line for the cashier. Wet Dream studied the young girl who was ringing people up. "This bitch better not ask for no ID to buy this blunt."

"Girl, why are you even buying that?" Shy asked. "I don't wanna hear Big Suga's damn mouth." When it was their turn and they stepped up to the register. "Can I get a single dutch?" Wet Dream asked. The voice they heard next made the hair stand up on the back of her neck.

"Oh, so we're smoking tonight?"

Wet Dream turned around slowly and couldn't help but bump into Big Suga standing only inches behind her and Shy. Big Suga made eye contact with the cashier and shook her head to let the girl know not to hand over the blunt. "You know that ain't happening. Not unless you buying that for me."

"Whateva, Suga." Wet Dream rolled her eyes and sucked her teeth.

"You got it twisted. You know smoking and business don't mix. That's a no-no, *ho!*" Big Suga shoved Wet Dream to the door and out into the parking lot. Shy looked around at the people who were whispering and pointing. She followed Big Suga and Wet Dream out the door without saying a word.

"Fuck, Suga! You ain't gonna keep putting your muthafucking hands on me!" Wet Dream spun around to face Big Suga once they were in the parking lot.

"Bitch, you got me fucked up! I'm gonna put more than these *muthafucking* hands on yo ass!" Big Suga kept pushing Wet Dream, causing her to stumble backward toward the car. "Much money as I spend on you bitches? And you wanna *talk back*?!"

"Oh hell…" Luscious sat in the passenger seat watching the fight and hoping it wouldn't get any more physical. She knew when Big Suga went inside the store to check up on the other two there was bound to be trouble.

"Bitch, all I know is you better make that money tonight!" Big Suga started to shove Wet Dream again but was stopped in her tracks when the girl suddenly pushed back.

"Suga, I told you! You ain't gonna keep putting your hands on me!" Wet Dream swung on Big Suga, and then kept swinging when Big Suga grabbed her around the shoulders and neck.

From across the parking lot, Kenya looked through binoculars at the two women tangled in a fight. "Heads up!" she said. "We got something. Cat fight."

Joe perked up. "What we got? Can you tell if one of them is Big Suga?"

"Looks like a match." Kenya watched for a few more seconds. "Yeah, that's her." She saw Big Suga spin the other woman around and kick her in the butt. Then, "Oh shit!" She and Joe both yelled inside the car as Big Suga pulled a gun from her purse. "I'm moving in, JoJo." Before Joe could object, Kenya eased her car door open and began moving closer to the action.

"Careful, Kenya! Watch out for that weapon," Joe whispered loudly to his partner. But it was obvious, neither of the women noticed Kenya closing in on them.

Big Suga pointed her gun straight at Wet Dream, who was inches away looking terrified with her hands in the air. "Don't you *ever* try to fuck my money up, bitch!"

"Tonya Day!" Joe called across the parking lot. He had gotten out of the car and was following Kenya. "Bounty hunter agent! We got a warrant for your arrest!" Both he and Kenya had their guns drawn. "Let me see those hands up! And get on your knees!" Joe kept barking commands while Kenya moved in from one side.

"Hell no!" Big Suga said, looking at Joe. Her gun was still pointed at Wet Dream. "I ain't going back! Got me fucked up. I got no love for her or nobody else! I'll kill this bitch first!"

"Put the gun down, Tonya. You don't wanna do it." Joe kept talking, trying to de-escalate the situation. Finally, Kenya moved to within a couple of feet from Big Suga and Wet Dream.

"Drop it, Tonya! Drop your weapon!" Kenya shouted. Stunned, Big Suga jerked around and her gun was suddenly pointed in Kenya's direction.

Pop! Pop! Two quick shots cracked the night air, and Big Suga fell like a sack of potatoes. "Oh my God!" Wet Dream cried and let out a loud scream. "No! No!"

"Don't move!" Kenya kept Wet Dream at bay while Joe rushed over to check Big Suga's vitals. Shy and Luscious watched in horror from inside the Cadillac. Their eyes were fixed on the body lying still on the ground. They couldn't imagine Big Suga not hopping right back on her feet. But no… when Joe touched her with the barrel of his gun, her body didn't move. In a matter of minutes, people started to gather around the scene. Kenya yelled for everybody to stay back.

"I'm calling 9-1-1. She's gone." Joe left the body and walked toward his partner. Everything had happened so fast, and he could see that Kenya was shaken. He tried to put her at ease. "Look, the gun is still in her hand. *And* we have witnesses. You did what you had to do. It's a wrap."

By this time, the *witnesses* – Shy, Wet Dream, and Luscious were pointing at Kenya and screaming profanity. Shy stepped forward and yelled, "You're going to pay for this! I don't care *who* you are! Rolling' through here with yo *fake ass* badge! Bullshit ass bounty hunter!"

"The three of you, stay back!" Joe warned.

"Naw, fuck that!" Shy raged on. "Trigger happy ho! Fake cop!" Wet Dream and Luscious just stood there stunned.

After a minute they just held each other, staring at Big Suga's body. But Shy had enough venom for the three of them. "What's your name, bitch?!" she continued to scream and point at Kenya.

"I got it, Joe." Kenya pulled out her phone. "Just make sure they stay back." She was about to dial for law enforcement, but stopped and finally turned her anger toward Shy. "Shut up… stupid hood rat! Your ass just got saved from years of torture. You just don't know. *Uugghh!*" She looked around at the crowd that had formed. "What's this address?"

"2234 Linden Road," one of the store employees called out.

"This is bounty hunter agent Kenya Wilson," she said into the phone. "I'm at 2234 Linden. I need police, an ambulance, and the crime scene unit at this location. Shots fired and one suspect down. Possible DOA. Okay…" she nodded her head at their response, "Copy."

"How long did they say it'll be?" Joe asked as soon as she ended the call.

"Dispatcher said about five minutes." The look on her face still showed all her tension and anxiety.

"Stay relaxed, Kenya," Joe spoke calmly to reassure her. "Like I told you, there was no other way to handle the situation. You didn't have a choice. She pointed a gun at you. Case closed, okay?" He nodded toward the three standing by the car. "Don't even bother responding to any of *that* shit. Just keep it professional. We got bigger things to tend to."

"I know, JoJo. It was either me or her, and she *wasn't* gonna be the one to come out on top. Plus, I l know we got a job to do."

"All the time."

*****

J was in the hallway upstairs and heard his brother E inside their bedroom making shooting sounds. *Pow!... Pow!* He walked into the room to see E using one of his pictures for target practice. It was a drawing of their school that J had taped to the wall over his bed. "Stop! Don't be doing that!" J shouted, jumping onto the bed to grab the picture and take it down.

"Come on J, let me have it for target practice."

"No way! I drew it for Mom."

"How come she don't have it then?"

"I'm giving it to her tonight."

"No, you not." E threw his toy gun to the side. "You lying. You just don't want me to have it."

"So what if you don't believe me? It's mine anyway!" E jumped up to try and grab his brother's drawing, but J jerked it out of his reach.

Rebbie walked into the room to see J giving his brother the coldest look she had ever seen one give the other. "Hey, hey! Y'all supposed to be in here cleaning up this room. What's going on?

40

Y'all in here fighting?" She looked back and forth between them, waiting for an answer.

"No, ma'am. We weren't fighting," E said. "J was just showing me a picture he drew for you. A picture of our school. Ain't that right, J?" He looked at this brother and smiled innocently.

"No!" J piped up, frowning at E. "He had his gun and was using it for target practice."

"Now wait a minute, E!" Rebbie walked in and stood between them. "Does your brother mess with your guns?"

"No, ma'am."

"Okay then. So don't you bother his drawings. Your brother like to draw, and you like to shoot."

"Okay, Mom. I'm sorry."

"Uh-uh… don't tell me sorry. Tell your brother."

"I'm sorry," E mumbled, looking at the floor.

"Say it loud so he can hear you," Rebbie insisted. "I heard your mouth all the way down the hall before I came in here."

"*I said I'm sorry,*" E said, looking up at J.

"Okay," J said, accepting his brother's apology.

"Now hand me my picture," Rebbie said and winked at J, "and finish cleaning up this room!" Just then, a sound from down the hall caught her attention and she went to the bedroom door to listen. "I think that's your father calling me. I'll be back," she said. "And have this room clean!"

While Rebbie was speaking, J slid his hand slowly across his bed to grab a pillow. As soon as she left the room, he yelled to his brother, "E!" and blindsided him with a swing to the side of the head.

"What!… Oh!" E yelled and fell onto his bed laughing.

"*Wham!* Too slow, man!" J doubled over laughing and didn't see E grab his own pillow. Soon, the argument over J's picture was forgotten as they laughed and chased each other around the room.

Rebbie reached the end of the hallway and walked into her bedroom to see Isaiah relaxing on the chaise lounge. "Daddy, did you call me?"

"I hear a lot of noise down there. What's them boys doing?" he asked.

"Supposed to be in there cleaning up that room. What's so funny?" she asked, noticing the amused look on her husband's face.

"Thinking about when E gets older. How I picture him being out in the field."

"He *might* want to do something different," Rebbie said.

"Umm… J maybe. But I know for sure E will wanna do this."

"Okay, Daddy. But what about your other son?"

"I see J being more reserved and to himself. More like a lady's man Isaiah looked at Rebbie and smiled. Getting a woman won't be hard, especially now in the nineties, with all these hot-tail little girls around."

"Oh no!" Rebbie protested. "We ain't having nobody knocking on my door talking 'bout we got twelve grandbabies out there!" She stepped in front of Isaiah, blocking his view of the television. "Daddy, you better teach that boy to keep his thing in his pants!"

"Aw baby, the boy gotta multiply… keep that name going. That's what the Lord wants."

"All I know is… with the cost of pampers, he better multiply that money before them babies!"

Chapter Five

E and Darius and their friend Rock sat on benches facing each other in the locker room. It was the end of the period, and the sound of voices and lockers slamming grew less as everybody else left the gym to get to their next class. "E, I know you gotta get on your knees and pray... I respect that. But you can't miss this party, man!" Rock used a towel to wipe his forehead.

"What are you saying, man?" E gave Rock a questioning look. "I pray three times every day, not just on Friday."

Rock lifted both hands in defense. "Nah, dog. I ain't challenging your religion. I'm just sayin'..."

"See you got it all wrong," E said. "Me and my folks ain't religious. We *spiritual*. There's a difference. Besides, I know how to serve the Father *and* these freaks!" he said with a sly grin.

"Whatever, man!" Rock laughed. "The baddest bitches gonna be up in the spot! And *shiiid*, don't forget about this..." E and Darius watched Rock reach and pull a huge blunt out of his bookbag. He sniffed it, and then waved it back and forth in front of them.

Darius clapped his hands together. "Let me get some of that fire, playa!" E fished in his pocket, pulled out a lighter, and handed it to Rock. He watched Rock light the blunt and then stood up. "I gotta go take a piss," he said and walked toward the urinals.

Rock took a long drag and then handed it off to Darius. "Yeah boy! This that shit right here!" Darius inhaled and then let off smoke in spurts. "Hell yeah, my nigga. Nothing but the best."

Up one flight of stairs a teacher, Mr. Dingles, walked a hallway and spoke to students during class change. "How was lunch today?" he asked one group of boys.

"Not good, Mr. Dingles," one student said, jokingly rubbing his stomach. "Don't eat the meatloaf!"

The teacher couldn't help but laugh along with the kids. "Alright, alright. Let's get to class," he said as the late bell rang. He turned to walk downstairs to the ground floor of the school, but stopped as a familiar odor met his nose and grew stronger. He followed the smell to the gym, and then into the boys' locker room. "*Well well well…* smells like we got some weed smokers!" He had walked through the door and right up to Darius and Rock without them even noticing. "I see where the party at!" Mr. Dingles stood glaring over the boys with his hands on his waist. "Y'all know we can't have this!" He looked at Darius. "Son, what's your name?"

"Da…Darius, sir." He looked at the joint in his hand, and then at Mr. Dingles. "I was just holding this for somebody."

"Just holding it, huh? Son, you gonna learn not to *hold* everything for everybody. If somebody cut off another person's head and asked you to hold it, would you do it? So, who are you holding it for… him?" Mr. Dingles nodded toward Rock, who had kept quiet the whole time. "If it's his, pass it back to him."

Darius wouldn't make eye contact with Rock, but reached out to try and hand him the blunt. Rock held his hands up and jerked away. "Man, what you doing?! That ain't mine! Don't be handing it to me!"

"Young man, what's your name?" Mr. Dingles asked Rock.

"Why you need to know my name? I'm just standing here talking." He kept his hands up and continued, "I don't have nothin' in my hands. You didn't catch me with *nothin'*."

Darius stared at Rock in disbelief, but turned when he heard E walking back in from the restroom. E was looking down straightening his clothes and talking, not paying attention to what he was walking up on.

"What's up, man! Y'all done smoked up all the weed?" When nobody answered, he looked up. "Oh man… *damn!*"

"Yep! Just like I figured," Mr. Dingles said with a satisfied grin. "Everybody, let's go! Straight to the principal's office."

*****

J and his girlfriend, Rachel, sat facing each other at a table to one side of the school cafeteria. Angela and two other girls sat watching them from across the room. "I sure hope she don't get pregnant by him," Angela said.

"Why you say that?" One of the other girls glanced in a mirror and then tossed it into her purse.

"'Cause she won't know if her baby will be moreno or blanco."

"Bitch, you sick! You sound crazy as hell," the other girl said.

"Really?" Angela rolled her eyes. "That boy got a twin brother and his ass is *white*," she said, enjoying the reaction from the other two at the table. "He cute though!" she giggled.

"Nah, no way!"

"Is so! Me and his brother E was both in Mrs. Paisley's class in the first grade. His Daddy and mama is all the way black. *And* they got cheese."

"Oh, so that bitch think she's slick. She trying to get her ass up in that money *quick*."

Rachel and J went on eating their lunch and talking about their classes. Rachel tapped the tip of one of her nails on the table.

"So… should I expect you to have a *normal* report for Black history?"

"I don't know about normal, but very informative," J answered. "I'm reporting on the 1906 Atlanta riots."

"The Atlanta riots? I never heard my grandparents talk about that."

"My Pops told me about it. A lot of black people died that day," J said.

"I wanna know more about it." Rachel leaned closer, waiting for J to continue.

"Man, I'm surprised your parents never told you about it," he said, forgetting his girlfriend's attitude toward certain words.

"*Man?* You see a *man* over here?" Rachel sat back, crossing her arms. She rolled her neck, holding back a smile.

"Come on, Rachel. You know I'm not coming at you like that. I'm sorry. I'm just feeling our conversation, that's all."

"Yeah, I know," Rachel answered sweetly. "I know you didn't mean any harm. I'm feeling it, too."

Across the room, Angela's phone vibrated. She grabbed it off the metal table to read the incoming text. "Ah Shit! Y'all still don't believe he got a white twin? Watch this," she said, getting up from the table. The two girls looked on as she walked over to J and Rachel's table. Angela swung her hair over one shoulder and cleared her throat. "Excuse me. I don't mean to interrupt y'all" she said, rolling her eyes at Rachel and then looking at J. "Your name J, right?"

"Why? Who's asking? Who are you?"

"Oh… I'm sorry. I'm Angela. Just thought I'd come let you know, your *white* twin brother and them just got caught blowing on some weed." The cafeteria was quiet, with everybody trying to see and hear what was going on.

"Wait… what is she talking about, J? You got a twin? And he's *white*?" Rachel asked, confused.

"Hold on, Rachel. Just relax." J reached out to hold her hand. Turning back to Angela he asked, "Why you saying my brother and *them*? Who is *them*?"

"Darius and Rock, that's who. Boy stop playing stupid, acting like you don't know." Angela swung her hair again, looking around and enjoying the attention from all the other tables in the room. But she took a step back and covered her chest when J suddenly stood up and got in her face.

"You better watch the lies you say about my brother, simple ass dummy!" He pointed a finger in Angela's face, careful not to actually touch her. Rachel sat frozen, trying to understand what was playing out in front of her.

Angela started to back away from the table. She shot a heated look in Rachel's direction. "Girl, you better be making sure that nigga *la correa*!" She sucked her teeth. "Strap up, 'cause you never know what you might get." Angela spun around and walked away, leaving J with flaring nostrils and balled up fists, and Rachel looking at him for answers.

*****

"The three of y'all sit right there." Mr. Dingles pointed to a set of chairs in the lobby of the front office.

"Mr. Dingles, I told you. I was just holding it. I wasn't smoking!" Darius continued trying to plead his case.

"Well son, you can explain that to the principal. Y'all boys stay seated while I go talk to Mr. Taylor." Mr. Dingles walked away, leaving E, Darius and Rock alone in the lobby. They immediately started to argue.

Rock glared at Darius. "Man, shut the fuck up 'fore I kick your ass!"

"Yeah man, that's what you *need* to do," E said, agreeing with Rock. "'Cause I was in the bathroom. And from what I saw, you didn't have it." He looked at Darius. "*You* did. So stop trying to sound all innocent. Just keep your damn mouth shut!"

"Dog, you know I ain't saying *shit*, Rock said. "Fuck snitching!" He bumped fists with E.

E looked at Darius, who had stopped talking and sat quiet, just staring at the floor. "Darius, you ain't gotta answer me. Long as you *heard* me."

In a separate wing of the school, J stood in front of his History class. He looked at Rachel, then at the rest of the students, and finally at his teacher. He cleared his throat and began:

My black history report is about the 1906 Atlanta Race riots.

W.E.B. DuBois, a black educator and writer, wrote a poem called 'Litany of Atlanta', calling on God for understanding and justice following the riots.

In the summer of 1906, the local Atlanta newspaper printed untrue accusations about black men assaulting white women.

On September 22, 1906, the false reports rallied thousands of angry white men who felt a need for killing – lynching any African American they came across.

The riot started in the Five Points section of the city and continued throughout the black business community, where

prominent black 44 business owners were murdered, and their
businesses were destroyed.
Innocent black men and women were pulled from streetcars
and stabbed with knives and pitchforks, their bodies strung up
and hung from light poles.
The massacre lasted for several days, with over 100 blacks
being killed.
Immediately following the riots, blacks fought hard for
human rights and equality that play an important role in our lives
today.
The 1906 Atlanta race riots is just one black historical event
out of many that was kept quiet and ignored for nearly a century.
I believe the importance of this event must be taught to
recognize the mistakes of white America in 1906, and to
acknowledge my ancestors who were killed because of the color
of their skin.
Thank you.

J's teacher walked forward and gave him a positive nod. "I like that, J. Very informative." She turned to the class. "Let's give J a hand." Rachel smiled and gave him two thumbs up while the other students applauded and said, "Good job!"

The Atlanta Race Riot of 1906

- Occurred Sept. 22-24, 1906 in downtown Atlanta

- White mobs killed dozens of blacks, wounded scores of others, and inflicted considerable property damage.

*****

Darius and his grandmother rode in silence. The school had called her to come pick him up. Every few seconds, she shook her head in disgust. "Son, if your mother was alive, she would back-slap you into next week! Smoking reefer!" She shifted in her seat behind the wheel. "I'm too old and weak to be trying to knock you down. 'Cause that's what you need!" She turned her angry face towards him. "Boy, don't you know when the white man lock your ass up, you're finished?!"

53

"I hear you, Grandma," Darius said, trying to sound cool. "But it is what it is. I ain't sweating nothing."

"Young ass smelling yourself. Sounding all proud… and *stupid!* What do you think your friends are gonna say when they find out you told on them?"

Darius shrugged and looked out the car window. "Whatever, Grandma. I get it from my Dad. Ain't that what you always say?"

The old woman looked at Darius again, surprised by his attitude. Gripping the steering wheel, she raised her eyes and lifted a sorrowful prayer, *"Oh Lord, I give him back to you! He's in your hands now. You are the only one that can straighten him out."*

Chapter Six

Rebbie was in her zone, moving around the kitchen preparing dinner, trying to get everything ready before Isaiah and the boys came home. Several pots simmered on the stove, filling the whole house with the smell of good food. She was taking some time to talk to Leah while she had the house to herself. "Hold on, girl. Let me put you on speaker." She took the phone from between her ear and shoulder and placed it on the counter. "Okay Leah, can you hear me?"

"Yeah, I hear you. Now, what were you saying?"

"Oh, nothing but I'm in here trying to get dinner ready. I had to start a little earlier than usual 'cause Isaiah called and said he's on his way home with E. I don't know what that's all about, but I *do* know them boys gonna be ready to eat up something soon as they come in!"

"Girl, I hear you! You over there like Betty Crocker," Leah laughed. "Yeah, you *better* have something ready for them hungry men when they come in!"

"*Ha ha...*" Rebbie said sarcastically but couldn't help but laugh. "But anyway, girl. Enough about me. What's going on with you these days? What's up with you and Ace?"

"Girl, we trying to work on a lil *somethin somethin.*"

"Alright then! Well, y'all keep working on a lil *somethin somethin.*" Rebbie turned from the stove and looked at the phone on the counter. "But Leah, tonight is the Lord's night... *no sex!*"

"Big Sis, *I know*. I won't let the father down."

"And…" Rebbie said, waving her mixing spoon as if Leah was in the room, "if he don't like it, you tell that coochie-hungry negro he's gonna stay hungry tonight!"

They both laughed. Then a timer went off, letting Rebbie know one of her dishes was ready. "Girl, let me get this food off the stove."

"Yeah, go and handle your business." "Just remember to discipline yourself, okay?"

"Ok, I will. Love you, Sis."

"Love you, too… later." Rebbie heard a car pulling up outside. Seconds later a door slammed, and she could see through the kitchen window that Isaiah had gotten out of the car. She walked outside to greet him in the driveway. "Hey!" she approached him with open arms, but the look on his face stopped her in her tracks. Past him, she saw E sitting in the passenger seat. "E! What you doing home? School don't let out at this time." She put her hands on her hips and shook her head, watching E as he sat still, not saying anything.

"Don't get quiet now!" Isaiah said loudly. "Get out and tell your mother how you like hanging out with potheads."

"Potheads?!" Rebbie looked from E to Isaiah, confused.

"No, it's not like that. I promise Mom," E said, getting out of the car. "I'm sorry." E looked at his mother, wishing he could take the disappointment from her eyes. He walked over and tried to hug her, but she shrugged him away.

"Nuh-uh! I don't want a hug from a son that ignores his responsibilities. I despise drugs!" Rebbie walked toward the house, but then turned around with balled fists. "As much as your Dad and I preach to you and J about staying away from that trash! And you go and get caught hanging around drug users! If you had brains, you'd be dangerous!"

E was hurt by his mother's words, but more so by how disappointed he knew she was. He didn't try to argue any further but hung his head and walked past her into the house. Isaiah had stood by to let Rebbie speak her peace but stepped forward to explain things as soon as E was inside. "Listen, Baby" he rubbed her shoulders, "they didn't find anything on E. He was actually using the restroom while two other boys were smoking. But… the school has a rule. If a student is caught near somebody using or selling, they get suspended, too."

"Okay, Daddy. I understand." She nodded, then looked up into his eyes with concern. "But who were the other boys? Does E know them?"

"Whether he know 'em or not, talking to our son and showing him what the scripture says is my concern right now."

"Ok, Daddy. Handle your son then." Rebbie stepped back and waved an arm toward the front door, then followed closely as Isaiah went into the house. She walked to the foot of the staircase and yelled for E while Isaiah sat down on the living room couch. "E!... Get down here!"

"Oh, you still got more questions to ask?"

"No, I just thought I'd call your son for you," she said to Isaiah.

E appeared on the landing and then walked past her into the living room. "Mom, I wasn't smoking. That's the truth." He raised his eyes to give Rebbie an honest look.

"I'm not having a weed head for a son!" she hollered.

"Rebbie! Let me…" Isaiah was beginning to raise his voice.

"Who were those other boys? Friends of yours?" Rebbie continued.

E hesitated, knowing he wouldn't lie to his mother about what happened and who he was with. "It was just Darius and…"

"Darius?!" she cut in. "You mean Darius that started the first grade with y'all?"

"Yes, ma'am."

"Humph! Darius… yeah, I remember him." She looked at Isaiah. "That boy didn't seem right way back then. Running off at the mouth. Calling somebody a liar."

Isaiah watched and listened as Rebbie and E went back and forth. He could tell when E was about to try and make a point. But he could hardly believe what came out of his son's mouth next.

"Mom, Darius' uncle said there"s nothing wrong with smoking weed! It's legal in California. Plus, some doctors say it's got medical benefits."

Isaiah stood up, unable to stay quiet any longer. "Boy! Go get the Bible! I know you probably thought weed wasn't in there."

Rebbie stared at E as he obeyed his father and went to bring a Bible from the nearby console table. "Hmph! I bet even Darius' uncle and them doctors don't know that. Bunch of flunkies."

"Turn to Genesis, chapter one, verse twenty-nine," Isaiah said and waited for E to find the passage. "What does it say? Read it out loud."

"And God said, I have given you every green herb that yields seed which is on the face of the earth, to you it shall be for food." E closed the book slowly and looked up at his father.

"You understand? Plain and simple." Isaiah looked at E and pointed to the book in his hands. "You eat it as food. You don't put fire to it. When you do that, you defile your body." He watched E's face as the truth was setting in. "

Wow! You wouldn't think the Bible talks about smoke."

"Yeah, son. It talks about everything young boys crave… money, sex, *and* drugs."

"And it's not called smoke," Rebbie added. "It's a *herb*."

"Okay, Mom. Can I get my hug now?" E gave his mother a pitiful look. "Sure, baby. You are the oldest and I love you." She reached for him with both arms and held him tight.

"I apologize for not using my best judgment. It won't happen again. I promise."

Later that night, E and J sat on the front steps, rehashing the events of the day. J shook his head in disgust. "Your boy Darius is a snitch."

This made E sit up straight. "What you saying?"

"What you mean, what I'm saying? How many weeks you out for?"

"Two," E shrugged like it was no big deal.

"Well, your boy only got a week." J cocked his head to one side, waiting for E's reaction.

"What?! Get the hell outta here!"

"Yep. I heard he snitched on Rock and told ol' crime dog Mr. Dingles that's where he got the weed from. Security came through with a locker sweep. They probably hit yours up, too. I *know* they found something in Rock's locker."

"Found what?" E asked.

"Man, what you think? Weed! I don't know how much, though."

"*Daaamn…* Darius went out like that? Busta muthafucker!" This time E shook his head in disgust. There was silence between the brothers until E's phone vibrated. He looked over his shoulder and said under his breath, "I just got a text from Rock. He's coming through."

"Bruh… after everything that went down, you still hangin' with that dude? And to make things worse, on the Sabbath?"

"I ain't got no problem with that man. His business is his business," E said.

"Man, *come on* E. You gotta be smarter than that. Today is rest day. Plus, you partying with smokers." J suddenly looked E in the eyes. "And what about you? Are you a blunt head now?"

"J, I swear… I never pulled on that blunt. I stepped off to take a leak, and when I came back, Crime Dog was right there. Darius was caught holding. That's how it went down."

J could see his brother was telling him the truth, and looked down with a nod.

"But," E continued, "when Pop showed me what God say about smoke, I was blown away!"

"Weed is in there?"

"Bruh, that's what I said!" E laughed, then looked at his phone when it vibrated again with another text. "Shit! Change of plans. I gotta go." He stood up from the steps and straightened his clothes. "Hit me up if anything pop off." He bumped fists with J, then jogged out of the front yard toward the street.

"Watch out for them connivers, bruh," J called after his brother.

E strolled casually down the street, and then turned a corner at the end of the block. After walking a little farther, he gradually made out the outline of Rock ahead of him, leaning against a car. The car was running, and the music inside was loud enough to shake the tinted windows. "Yo, white boy! What's up!" Rock stepped forward to give E some dap but stopped when he saw E's expression.

"Who the fuck you calling white? My daddy Black cuz… don't get it twisted!" E's fingers were balled into fists, and he looked ready to square up. But he calmed himself down, remembering why he was there. He nodded towards the car. "Darius up in there?"

"Yeah, he's in there," Rock said. "Just be cool, nigga. Since you ain't *white,*" Rock said and laughed to himself.

"I'm not no nigga either!" E said, his anger building again.

Rock stared at E for a second, sizing him up, but then decided to stand down. He shook his head and waved a hand. "Anyway, dog. *Whatever.*"

E opened the door behind the driver and got into the car. Black, an older guy from the neighborhood, was in the driver's seat horsing the engine. Lights from the street made the dark ink from Black's neck and face tattoos stand out. The swirling pattern caught E's eye, and he tried to make out the design.

Darius sat on the opposite side of the back seat. He was leaning back into the darkness of the corner. "What's up, E?"

"What's up," E said without looking in his direction. "*Shiiit…* just ready for this party. Gotta get my dick wet, that's all," Darius said with a cocky grin.

In the front seat, Rock hit Black's arm and pointed at E. "This my folks. That's E."

"What's up, folk. I'm feeling them tatts," E said. "Sup, playa. 'Preciate it." Black looked at E in the rearview mirror and nodded.

"How much time you got, E? From that shit that happened today," Rock asked.

"Two weeks," E said. He looked over at Darius who was quiet and stone-faced.

"Yeah? Darius only got one." Rock looked straight ahead and sucked his teeth. "Maaan… it was crazy!" He pounded the armrest. "I'm out for the rest of the year. Plus, I got arrested!"

"Get the fuck outta here! How you get arrested?"

"Man, I lie to you not… especially on the Sabbath. Them niggas went to searching lockers. They search yours?"

"I don't know," E said. "My Pops came and got me."

"I don't know, either. I left with my grandma," Darius said.

There was a long silence after Darius spoke. Then Rock looked at Black. "Cuz, they found two ounces in my shit."

"Lil nigga, *why* would you keep that in your locker?" Black shook his head.

"Waiting on Fatso ass to pick it up," Rock said. "Now I got this damn court date. And then rehab on top of that… *maybe*." Rock looked out his car window. "Probably that nigga Lil Bo that snitched. Yeah…" He turned and looked at E. E looked at Darius.

Black horsed the engine again before pulling away from the curb. "I gotta make a pit stop. Then the party. Them hos can wait. I'm 'bout my paper." After a few miles, Black pulled over to a convenience store and stopped in the parking lot. He flashed his lights, then waited as a man jogged toward them from across the street.

Rock asked Black, "You know this dude?" But he only received a look that told him not to ask any more questions.

"Man, I've been calling you back-to-back. Why you ain't been picking up? Everything good?" Black eyed the man who was now standing beside the car.

"Yeah, everything straight, cuz." The man pulled an envelope from his jacket and handed it to Black.

Black quickly looked at the envelope and then back at the man standing outside his open window. "Look like my paper is all here," he said, "but cuz, I got no need for sneaky individuals like you."

"What you saying, bruh?" The man looked nervous. "Where is all this coming from?"

"Answer the phone when grown folks call!" The man barely took a step back, with his eyes wide and hands in the air when two shots rang out. He doubled over and fell to his knees after being shot at point-blank range. Tires squealed as Black sped away. Inside the car, the music was still bumping, and Rock, E, and Darius sat stiff and quiet, not believing what had just happened.

E was the first to break the silence. "Oh shit!"

Then Darius started hysterically, "Oh my God! He just shot that nigga!"

"Yo cuz, did you have to *shoot* him?" Rock asked. "That four-fifth ain't no joke! He ain't getting up from that!" E shouted.

Black kept driving, not feeding into the excitement. Staring at the road ahead, he said in a cool tone, "When a man give another man the chance to put loot in his pocket, that's a good thing."

"For sure," E spoke up from the back seat. "Not many recognize that."

"See! Now that's what I'm saying!" Black looked at Rock. "Your boy E here understands that time is money. So… when *I* call, pick up the fucking phone! See, when you ignore me, it feel like my shit ain't important or like I don't exist. So, I make that person nonexistent. Feel me?" He looked around at everybody in the car.

"I feel you, cuz. That's what's up," Rock answered.

Darius spoke up, still shook. "Dog… I don't know about this. What if the store had cameras? I can't go to jail," he said, sounding like a little kid.

"Jail? Where you coming from?" E looked Darius up and down. "I hear you running your mouth, once again."

"Man, I want out. Let me out this car!"

"Ain't nobody bouncing out this car, so kill that noise, young nigga!" Black continued to drive.

Rock reached into his pocket and brought out two blunts. "All yours, cuz," he said and gave one to Darius. "Shut up and spark up! I got my own." He watched in the side view mirror as Darius lit up. "Yeah… calm your nerves, cuz." It wouldn't be long before the poison in the blunt would start to take effect.

"E, you wanna hit this?" Darius offered E a drag.

"Hell nah, don't pass me shit! That strong drink is all I want!"

Darius kept pulling on the joint, bobbing his head to the music and waiting for the calming effect of the weed to kick in. "This shit is hitting, Rock!"

"Yeah… hit it, my nigga!" Rock watched him take another deep hit, then start coughing and punching his chest.

"I need to put this shit out! Got me sweating, bruh." Darius stared at the blunt and shook his head.

"Nah, don't put it out. That shit is teaching you a lesson. Got you weak… Pussy!" Rock said as he and Black exchanged a look.

"Man, my shit racing! Damn… it's hot in this muthafucker!"

E could see that Darius looked scared. "You alright, dog? Look like you trying to be a grown man and can't handle it."

"Oh man, I'm dizzy… damn!" Darius's voice was shaking.

"Rock, what you got D smoking on?" E could see Darius needed help, but he didn't know what to do, or if he should even touch him.

"Same thing from earlier," Rock answered calmly from the front seat, pretending not to notice Darius's reaction to the weed.

"Whatever it is, this snitch is sweating!"

"Man… I ain't no snitch! Say what you want!" Darius was still pounding on his chest and sounding like he was about to choke.

He hit the back of Black's headrest and said, "Black, drop me off up here at the hospital. My heart feel like it's 'bout to bust out my chest. Fuck a party!"

Black yelled from the front seat, "Fuck going to Emergency! I'll drop you down the block, and that's all I'm doing!"

"Oh man, Rock. What was in that shit?"

"You deaf, nigga?" Rock turned to Black. "Cuz… hurry up and get this green ass nigga outta here!"

Black stomped on the brake and swerved to the side of the street. "Get out, man! Grady is down the block."

"Nah, man, pull up," Darius pleaded. He was doubled over, and his voice was muffled from behind the front seats.

"Get out! Busy talking when you could'a been down the block," Black shouted over his shoulder.

Darius stumbled out of the back passenger-side door and slammed it behind him. He stumbled forward a few steps, then fell onto the sidewalk holding his chest. As soon as the door slammed, Black sped off. "That's what happens to snitches! They never see it coming!" E yelled over the music.

"Fuck that herb-ass nigga!" Black kept driving. "You young niggas need a woman tonight… not no lil high school hoes. And I got the right party for y'all." About ten minutes later, they turned into a neighborhood on the outskirts of town. Black slowly steered the car up a long driveway until they were parked in front of a mansion.

"Damn, cuzzo! This the party?" Rock looked from side to side across the parking pad. "Benzos and Bentleys all up in the spot! Who crib?"

"This my man T-Man's spot," Black said. "And I hope you niggas ain't the quiet type, 'cause these honeys ain't having it."

"Super bad divas, huh?" E asked from the back seat. "What you know about divas, E?" Black teased. "Stick 'em hard and leave 'em where they lay!"

"Word up! 'Cause these hoes will put your rod in their mouth with no problem," Black said.

"That's what it is then." Rock opened his door to step out. "We grown men."

Black went first as they walked through the heavy wood doors of the mansion. He led them straight through the crowd of people gathered right inside. They were allowed through a set of double doors into the VIP room. E and Rock kept their cool but couldn't stop looking around at the beautiful women in sexy outfits. Like Black said, these were grown women, not any "lil high school hos." Some were standing in groups holding drinks and dancing to the music. Some smiled and nodded to the men who were chatting them up. And some were giving lap dances, like this badass chick who was pleasing a dude on a couch right inside the doors.

At the back, a man sat watching everything going on in the room. A huge dude named Heavy stood at his back, also scanning the room and everything going on. Heavy leaned down to hear his boss T-Man saying, "Nothing more important than loyalty. No matter the situation." Heavy stood up straight and started to move forward when he noticed three guys walking toward the boss. But T-Man stood to greet them. "Black! My lil soldier!" He turned to Heavy and said, "Now, loyalty runs in this young man's veins."

"Boss Man, you know this young nigga like that?" Heavy eyed Black, Rock and E suspiciously, sizing them up.

"Some people you feel sure about. Especially when they know who the enemy is and how we work. Black knows this. Just like Keke over there giving that man a dance." T-Man waved toward the chick they had noticed by the door. "See how she got him smiling? She know that smile is coming, so she trusts in what she do."

"Hey, T-Man. This my folks, Rock and his partner E." The boys nodded and said, "What's up."

T-Man surprised E by addressing him directly and asking, "What kind of woman would you consider her to be?" He pointed to the woman he called Keke.

"A harlot," E said.

"This young man getting biblical over here!" T-Man laughed.

"She can repent. But if not, that's what she will be. A lil black ho."

"True," T-Man said. "I can understand that. But Keke won't change... at least not tonight. Tonight, she want something different."

"I can see that Boss Man," E nodded. "Call me T-Man."

"No problem… T-Man."

"Hope not, 'cause Keke want something different *in* her tonight. Feel me?"

"You ain't said nothing but a nice word. Nice meeting you," E said.

"Be easy, man. We'll talk again." T-Man reached out to pump fists with E.

"For sure."

T-Man made eye contact with Keke, and without saying a word she ended her dance and walked straight to E. Taking his hand, she led him toward a closed door at the back of the room.

"Damn! Hey girl, my time up?" the man who had been enjoying her assets called behind her.

"Yes it is," she said, walking through the door with E and then closing it behind them.

"Hey! One of you ladies get over here and take care of my young guest," T-Man called out in the room. Rock took a seat on the sofa, grinning as another female came over and sat on his lap.

*****

Isaiah blessed the food as the family sat around the breakfast table. Afterwards, his eyes rested on E. "Don't think your mother and I forgot about your suspension. No laying around and sleeping all day. I got things for you to do around the house."

"And I'm making sure of it," Rebbie said.

"Come on, Mom," E whined.

"What?" Rebbie cut her eyes. "Don't forget, people who associate with weed smokers *stay* on punishment in this house."

"What in the world…" They all turned to look at the television as Isaiah turned up the volume. He shook his head. "Another body."

The family was silent listening to a local reporter, Charles Gibson, reporting from a scene near downtown.

"A body was found in the parking lot of this convenience store in the southeast section of Atlanta. It is believed to be a Black male who was shot. Police have no suspects at this time. Charles Gibson reporting."

"I tell you what…" Isaiah said, turning back to the table, "I'm tired of seeing Black men have no respect for life." E stared into his plate and continued stuffing his mouth with food.

"I need to write about that. Brothers killing brothers. What you think, E?" J looked at his brother but didn't get an answer. He pushed E's shoulder to get his attention.

"Nothing man, nothing." E turned to Isaiah and asked to be excused from the table. "I'm not feeling too well."

Rebbie studied her son as he got up from the table. "What's wrong with you, E?"

"I don't know, Mom. All of a sudden, my stomach is acting up."

"Eating too fast. The food don't have feet. Take your time, boy!"

"I know, Mom." E picked up his plate to take it to the sink. "J, come to my room when you finish."

"Okay, bruh. But give them eggs up. I got a place for 'em." He motioned for E's plate before he left the table.

"That boy's eyes is bigger than his belly," Rebbie said and shook her head.

Upstairs in his bedroom, E sat on the side of his bed, talking to Rock on the phone. "Yeah, I saw it. Shit is real, dog."

"No doubt. That's why I asked cuz why he shot him. We better get us an alibi," Rock said.

"Yeah, working on that right now."

"You coming out tonight?" Rock asked.

"I don't know, why?" E asked, though he already knew his answer was a negative.

"Make some power moves with Black."

E twisted his face and looked at the phone. He was surprised Rock wasn't planning to lay low, especially for now. "Nah man, I'm chilling for the next couple of weeks. You need to do the same, dog."

"Can't do it, man. I'm chasing paper," Rock said. "Shit man," E said and rubbed his head, "just watch yourself." He heard a knock on the door and remembered he asked J to come to his room. "Gotta go, bruh. I'll holla at you."

J knocked again and then walked into the room. Seeing E's tense expression, he laughed. "What's going on with you? Eating that coochie got your stomach hurting?" He took a playful swing at his brother. "You know Pops taught us not to eat anything that gets up and walks away."

E couldn't help but laugh. "You sound crazy! I was smashing last night," he said, stroking his chin.

"What, six packs?" J teased.

"Hell nah, I was drinking that hen dog. *Hennessey.* Big dog liquor. Then I had this super bad shorty giving me brains the whole night. Nonstop. I bust off and she'd get right back on the job."

"Dang, bruh! Freaky girls like *that* was at his party?"

"This was another spot, J. Rich folk and older broads with deep throats," E boasted. "But that's not what I need to tell you." All of a sudden, his smile disappeared and the expression on his face was dead serious. "Close the door."

"What?" J closed the door and locked it. "You got a problem with somebody? Who is it?"

"Nah, nothin' like that, lil bruh. You know I can take care of myself. It's got to do with what you just saw on the news."

J had a blank look at first, but then his eyes got wide. "Man, you *killed* somebody?!"

"Keep your voice down, J!"

"Brother, tell me you don't have nothing to do with that. Pops is gonna *kill* you!"

"No, man. Do I look like I'd kill somebody?"

"I don't know. I didn't think my older brother would be hanging with blunt heads either, so…"

"Listen, I ain't here to talk about what a person might do, but what somebody *did*." E sat looking at the floor for a few seconds, and then looked his brother in the eyes. He slowly began re-telling everything that happened the night before. J sat down next to him, listening and trying to take it all in. He was surprised at how calm and monotone E's voice sounded. J couldn't tell whether his brother understood the seriousness of the situation. "So that's what happened," E said. "Rock's cousin just shot a dude and drove off."

"I got a question. Was Darius with y'all?" J raised his eyebrows, waiting for the answer.

Without hesitation, E rattled off the answer he had already rehearsed in his head. "Nah, I last saw Darius at school yesterday when all that other stuff went down."

"That's a good thing. 'Cause if he was there, you'd have a lot more to worry about," J said.

"Yeah, I know." E put an arm around his brother's shoulder. "Seem like I'm always in the wrong place at the wrong time. I need you, lil bruh. Out of all the things we shared between us, this is serious. Don't say shit to nobody."

J looked at E and laughed a little. "The older brother is always coming to the younger. You ain't gotta worry 'bout that. I won't say nothing."

"If anybody ask my whereabouts last night, I was home. Bet?" E gave his brother a serious look.

"You sure are asking a lot." J sat looking back at his brother. "You need to come with something valuable… for all that."

"Name it, J. Whatever you want me to do. 'Cause I'm kinda worried 'bout this murder. Not to mention me doing prison time."

"You better worry 'bout Pops beating your ass," J said, lifting his eyebrows.

"Damn J, I'm serious! Stop with the games, man!" "Alright then…" J tapped his chin like he was deep in thought, "tell you what. Your right to the family business. Sign it over to me."

"Okay! If that's what it takes." E appeared to be relieved at what seemed like such a small request. "But," he looked at his brother and asked, "are you sure you can do the job? Chasing gangsters and being' in shootouts like Pops and Uncle Joe?"

"I don't see me having any problems," J said, sounding cocky. "Just hand me a sheet of paper, so we can make this a done deal."

E went to a notebook on his dresser and pulled out a clean sheet of paper. He gave it to J along with a pen. He stood back and watched J write out an agreement, but after a couple of minutes he was impatient. "Okay, man let me hear what you got," he said over J's shoulder.

"Give me a second. I'm almost finished… what's today's date?"

"Twenty-third," E answered. He watched J draw a line across the bottom of the page and write the date beside it.

"Okay, here it is," J turned around and started to read what was on the sheet of paper. "I, E Jones, on this twenty-third day of February 2005, give my inheritance, slash, all ownership of family business to J. Jones." He handed the paper to E, who quickly looked it over. "We straight?" J asked.

"If you say so." E shrugged and signed his name on the agreement.

"I'll make you a copy," J said and took the piece of paper.

"Yeah, you do that lil bruh." E went to his bed and reached underneath to pull out a hunting rifle. He turned to J with a slight smirk on his face and held the gun out to him. "Well, now I think you better do less writing and more shooting."

"Don't worry," J said. "I'll be able to do both. I'll be sharp with the pen and the gun."

Chapter Seven

The woods around the field were quiet, except for the birds in the trees. Isaiah, Joe, and the twins crouched low in the brush, out of sight of a small buck grazing about a thousand feet away. Isaiah spoke in a low and steady tone to J, who had his rifle scope fixed on the deer. "Steady… keep it steady, son. Don't rush it. Don't take your eyes off him. Okay, son… take the shot." A loud crack of gunfire broke the quiet in the woods and caused the birds overhead to squawk and fly in a frenzy.

"Damn! Just a little off!" J cussed.

"Come on, bruh. Step up your game! How you miss him?" E laughed, teasing his brother.

"Man, I don't know how I missed that kill! Guess I rushed it," J said.

Isaiah slapped J on the back. "Still a good shot, son. You kept your poise, and that's what matters."

"That bad boy ducked the other way at the last second!" Joe walked up to J and patted him on the shoulder.

"Well… I woulda' took the shot a lot quicker," E said.

"Okay then son, show him how it's done," Isaiah said to E.

"I will," E said, staring J in the eye. "You don't have to tell me when to shoot." The boys locked eyes for several seconds until E walked away.

"Yeah, okay… Mr. PlayStation," J mumbled under his breath. He and Joe looked at each other and chuckled as they walked toward Isaiah and E. They stopped in their tracks when Isaiah suddenly signaled up ahead. They could hear him speaking to E in a loud whisper.

"Look straight ahead. You see him? It's the same one."

But E shook his head and pointed to his left. "Look to the left, Pop. I see one a whole lot bigger."

"Yes sir… granddaddy buck! Look every bit of two hundred." Isaiah made a motion for Joe and J to catch up. "What you figure, Joe?"

"Oh yeah, that's a big son of a gun," Joe said, walking up slowly to stand beside Isaiah. He squinted at E. "Can you handle it?"

"Watch this… we eating deer tonight. I got the drop on him, Unc." E steadied his grip and aimed the rifle.

"Take that deep breath." Isaiah's voice was steady and low.

E drew in a long, deep breath and held it. "Goodnight." Another loud blast shook the woods, and they watched the buck fall like a sack of potatoes.

"Yes!" E lowered the gun and pumped his fist. "I got him, Pop! Dropped him where he stood!"

"Good shot, son! There you go! Now that's my boy right there!" Isaiah and E locked eyes and did a fist bump.

"See… I told you! I was born to do this!" E held his arms out wide, welcoming the praise. Isaiah and Joe exchanged wide grins and slapped each other five. In all the excitement, J's somber expression went unnoticed.

*****

A gathering of family and friends Angela, Rachel, Annette, E and J homeboys were assembled in the family garage celebrating the twins' 21st birthday, bobbing their head to 'In Da Club'. Angela stood up to dance for E. "Yeah…that's right! It's your birthday, baby! We gonna party like it's your birthday! Heeey!"

"She ain't even doing that right." Another friend, Annette, walked up beside Angela and started to swirl her hips. "Let me show her how to do it." E and J and the rest of the fellas looked on, enjoying the music and the live show.

Inside the house, a group of older women had taken over the kitchen table and seats around the island. Leah waved her hand to get Kenya's attention. "Kenya! Girl… what you doing to keep that weight down?"

"Child… running after criminals! And you can blame her husband for that," Kenya said and jokingly rolled her eyes in Rebbie's direction as the other women laughed.

"Oh no," Rebbie said, "Joe is the one! He the fitness trainer. When Joe says 'Kenya it's time to move…' oh boy, sista be on it!"

"Well…" Kenya shrugged and laughed.

Another lady at the table stretched her eyes, looking surprised. "Oh my! So… you're a bounty hunter?"

79

"Yes, I'm a bounty hunter," Kenya answered. "And I love my job." She looked the woman squarely in the face.

Leah cut in, feeling the tension in the room. "Is something wrong with that? Is that a problem?" she asked the woman.

"Oh, not at all," the woman replied, nervously stroking her bleached blonde hair and patting the skin around her freckled nose. "I just wasn't expecting that. I'm sorry if you took it that way," she apologized to Kenya. "We all must do God's work in one form or fashion."

While the woman spoke, Leah eyed her from head to toe, sizing her up. She knew that Rebbie and Isaiah's circle of friends included all kinds of people, but she couldn't remember ever sitting around Rebbie's table with anybody of the Caucasian persuasion. "So… what's your occupation?" Leah asked the white woman.

"Oh, I'm sorry!" She extended her hand. "I'm Mrs. Wallace, First Lady of the First Baptist Church. How do you do?" When Leah didn't reach forward, Mrs. Wallace pulled back her hand and placed it over her chest. "My husband, Pastor Wallace, is a close friend of Isaiah's. They been knowing each other for years."

"Oh yeah? That's interesting." Leah sucked her teeth. "But again, what's your occupation? I mean, besides being a high-privilege white woman married to a brother." The kitchen went silent, and the pastor's wife looked confused. Everyone was either staring at Leah in disbelief or watching Mrs. Wallace, waiting for her reaction.

"Uh… Roxy honey!" Rebbie stood abruptly and broke the silence. She reached for a metal tray that was covered with aluminum foil. "Will you take this out to Mr. Jones for me?"

"Yes, ma'am." Roxy was younger than the twins and their other friends, but had made herself comfortable with the older women inside the house. She usually enjoyed the real grown woman talk, but at that moment was more than happy to escape the brewing drama. She grabbed the tray and headed toward the patio. She could hear Isaiah's voice bragging, "That chicken smelling good!" and saw him walking toward the door.

"Just set that on the table by the grill… thank you," he said, pointing to a patio table when he passed Roxy in the doorway.

"Okay," she said sweetly and smiled. Walking toward the table, Roxy noticed another man sitting in a chair on the patio. It was Pastor Wallace.

"God has surely blessed you with a pretty face," he said. "Thank you."

"You in college?" he asked, leaning forward in his chair.

"No, I'm just fifteen." Roxy turned toward him and immediately saw that his eyes were roaming from her face to the rest of her body.

"Nothing like that young flesh to caress," he said with a toothpick to one side of his mouth. "Can I get a name and number?

Or am I out of place asking you something so personal?" he asked, lifting an eyebrow.

"Not really." She put a hand on her hip and rolled her body to one side. "But… that comes with a price."

"Umph!" The pastor grunted and shifted in his seat. "Pastor can afford anything God brings his way. Especially potential," he said with a sleazy grin.

"Okay then." Roxy walked a couple of steps forward so she wouldn't have to raise her voice. "4-0-4, 5-4-5, 7-8-5-5. Roxy... You got it?"

"A man of God remembers things of importance, Miss Roxy."

"Is that right?"

*****

In the garage, E sat on a bench with Angela on his lap. She smiled and moaned lightly as he rotated kisses between her neck and lips. Across the floor, J sat at a small folding table with Antonio, Ben, Rachel, Chris and Annette. "So, you speak the word?" Antonio asked Annette.

"We all speak that conscious, militant word for our brothers and sistas," she answered.

E turned his attention away from Angela and joined the conversation. "You like spitting that rough, rugged and raw shit, huh?"

"Depends on who or what, feel me? I'm just for my people."

Antonio rubbed both hands down his face and laughed. "Well E, that leaves us and Angela out!"

"Aw shit," J said, rolling his eyes. "Here we go with this nonsense. A lot of your Latin brothers don't have love for us blacks... but you kiss blanco ass. You better wake up."

E suddenly stood up to confront Antonio. "Who the fuck is this, yo?! We both came out my Dad's nut sack… We hebrews from shem!" He stepped toward Antonio. "I may look white on the outside, but I'm chosen. Don't get it twisted!"

"Damn, E! Calm your nerves, I was just shooting Annette a question." Antonio leaned back with both hands in the air.

"Just don't shoot too many my way," Annette said.

Ben, in his Jamaican accent asked, "Wah not?"

"What the hell, homeboy speaks?!" Chris busted out laughing.

"Fuck dee jokes, mon! Shorty was saying sumtin," Ben said.

"Yo cuz, watch your word play up in here! No need to come like that," J yelled.

Just like Antonio, Ben leaned back and held up his hands. "Easy J! Me jus' trying to find out what baby girl got to say."

"Yeah well, kill that noise, 'cause speaking out of pocket can cause a problem," E warned.

"Yeah, that's right." J stared at Ben, nodding in agreement with his brother.

Beep! Beep! A car horn from out in the street broke the tension. "Oh shit, that's my folks," E said. "I'll be back." He pulled up on his belt and walked out to where Rock was parked on the curb.

"What's up, birthday boy?" Rock reached out and slapped five with E through the window.

"Just enjoying my day," E said with a shrug. "What's up, dog?"

"You know… doing what I do," Rock said. "But listen up. T-Man need to holla at you."

"For what?"

"Your crew got people talking."

"You know me," E said. "I don't give a damn 'bout people talking."

"Word is, you got the burbs on lock. Getting that extortion money from them Arabs. T-Man admires that shit, dog."

Before E could respond, Rebbie walked out onto the porch and called to him. "Come on in and cut the cake, 'cause your daddy is ready to eat! Tell your friend to come on in. He's welcome."

"Nah, he alright, Ma," E answered over his shoulder. Rebbie stood on the porch wiping her hands on a kitchen towel, trying to see who E was talking to. "Tell him to park that car and come get something to eat," she yelled across the yard.

E waved over his shoulder and then turned back to Rock. "Tell T-Man to give me a couple of hours. I got some cake to eat."

"That's a bet, white boy," Rock said and nodded with a sly grin.

"I told you once already 'bout calling me a white boy. One day you might pay for the name-calling."

"That's a threat, dog?" Rock shifted in his seat and shot E a menacing look.

"You heard me clear. I didn't stutter."

Just as quick, Rock's expression went from threatening to amused. "So, it's like that when you get to be the big man?" He looked at E and laughed. "I didn't come over here to beef with you. I'm just the messenger, feel me?"

"Yeah, whateva Rock. I'll holla at him." E hit the bottom of the window and stepped back from the car. Rock locked eyes with E for a few seconds before punching the gas. There was a loud screech and the smell of burnt rubber when he drove off.

Inside the house, the sound of Stevie Wonder singing Happy Birthday filled the family room. E walked in and stood beside J while everybody else celebrated and sang along. Isaiah and Rebbie stepped out and turned the center of the room into a dance floor, waving for others to join them. Pastor Wallace stood directly behind his wife while she watched the dancers. His eyes were searching along the wall on the other side of the room until they landed on Roxy. He openly stared, hoping to get her attention.

*****

The standing-room-only crowd waited patiently between poets in the dimly lit club. This Friday, J, Rachel, Annette, and Chris were among the crowd. The chatter subsided as soon as the emcee walked back into the spotlight at the front of the room. Adjusting the microphone with one hand, he leaned forward to announce the next artist. "Made some folks mad the last time on stage," he chuckled. "Coming out the ATL… Decatur where it's greater… Give it up for J!" J made his way through the crowd and stepped on stage. He stood staring over the crowd for a few seconds before he began.

Death is spreading with the quickness, climbing the charts
Brothers yelling, let's get it on!
Once the guns bust it's a wrap. Dust to dust
Spirits go back to the father is a must. He who orchestrates it all.
Judgement you can say, 18-year-old hit by a stray.
Teenage male been here before, three to four generations ago
Probably a woman beater or took pleasure shooting people with the heater.
The Lord is escalating things no matter your feelings or thoughts, last days!
Final call for the unjust, that hour cometh when many will be caught up in lust
Living on the left side, too many immoral deeds recorded throughout your personal history.

I rejoice when the wicked is punished, sigh and cry when the rich oppress the poor. Keeping it real, dog, are men who kneel and pray willing to walk in truth no matter what the two-third say?

Denounce all lies. Pay attention to the signs, realizing everything has an opportune time.

God is love and hate, war and peace, a killer and a healer.

He controls it all, even Satan. Best believe he knows the ones who faking.

My people show what dominates they brain. Adultery, money and cars, which are all vain Teach what is what to the young, so little girls won't grow up being sluts and little boys would know when to put away toys

Myself being a slave for holiness, knowing the black man is the prey, I'm built for this Michael and Gabriel – angelic generals protect me

Many Americans is way off point, having faith in your religious views, believing what pastor taught is the correct news, thinking all flesh would be saved, designed to deceive the masses with tricks when preparation should be the topic, getting your life in order

Repent and turn from your wicked ways because the day would soon be here, spiritual warfare!

My big brother Jesus Christ came not for peace, but death

Only the one-third and his elect would be the only ones left.

The room had been silent, except for the snare drum and horn keeping a steady beat while J's words spilled out over the audience. Then, several seconds after his last line, Rachel and everyone else broke into thunderous applause. Whistles and hand claps filled the air, along with the traditional finger snaps.

Chapter Eight

E sat in a straight-back chair in front of a carved wood desk with T-Man on the other side. "Relax, man! I just wanna talk to you," T-Man teased when he noticed E looking around at the bodyguards and flunkies in the room. "I hear you doing good, man. Giving them Arab muthafuckers hell."

"Somebody gotta make 'em pay. When you clearing half a million a month on Blacks and Mexicans, and you ain't trying to share with the poor folks that's filling your pockets." E sucked his teeth. "That's robbery. Feel me?"

T-Man sat with his fingers locked, listening and nodding. "We on the same page, lil bro. I admire your spirit, for a young hustler going after them big muthafuckers." He leaned forward behind the desk and pointed a finger at E. "I could use you on my team. We could add a lot more store owners to the list."

"Nah, I'm good, T-Man. I'd rather have a short list. I was taught… take your time and watch how you step." E watched T-Man's smile turn to a look of disappointment.

"Be for real! Whatever you clearing now, that shit can triple with no problem!"

"True… but this hustle is wide open. Nobody in the A is running this caper. No disrespect, but I like calling the shots. Taking orders ain't for me."

"See, I knew we was cut from the same cloth. I refused to take orders when I was young, too." T-Man scratched at the stubble on his chin. "Doing six years for robbery made that hard. Damn guards telling you when to eat and wash your ass. So, never say what you can't do. I had to adapt. But once I was out…" he turned his plush leather chair from side to side, "… sold dope, robbed some other muthafuckers… and I peeped that pussy don't ever play out. So I started my escort service."

"It paid off, right?" E asked. "You living off the fatness."

"Hell yeah!" T-Man laughed and looked around at his lavish surroundings. "I'm just greedy." He stopped laughing and studied E for a second. "Let me ask you a question. You been hanging out with Black folks your whole life, how do your old man people feel about it?"

"What you mean by that?" E asked, confused.

"My dad is white, and my mom is Black," T-Man started to explain, "so I caught a lot of shit from my dad's side of the family. You know… *'What you doing hangin' out with them black boys? You gonna follow them niggas straight to prison.'* Trust me, I heard it all."

"Well, my dad is Black," E said.

"Oh, okay! So, Pops married a white woman?"

"Nah, my mama Black, too." E was amused by the confused look on T-Man's face.

"What…you adopted?"

E shook his head. "I'm a twin. My brother has black skin."

"You a twin? Damn, that's wild… some Esau and Jacob shit!"

"Yeah, I heard that before," E said. "I learned to live with it. God does what he wants."

"I see," T-Man said, looking impressed. "It made you a big man, and it shows. I peeped that when I met you a few years ago. Just don't get too big and start stepping on my toes. That wouldn't be Kosher."

"No need for the hard talk. I teach my soldiers to stay in their lane. I just expect the same from you and your crew."

"My dogs only bite when I tell 'em to." By now, T-Man and E were exchanging serious, unblinking stares.

*****

Rock pulled hard on a blunt and then passed it to his partner, Dino. "Fucking white boy E really think he the shit. I put his ass on when we was young as hell. Muthafucker all proud now 'cause he making that paper." The air inside the car was filled with grey smoke, and Rock choked on his words.

Dino squinted through the smoke and handed the joint back to Rock. "Give the word, bruh. I'll run up on him with the burner, cuz."

"Nah, don't fuck wit' him. He still got a pass," Rock said. "I'll let you know if shit changes."

"You know me, nigga. I love taxin' a cracker. Fuck how they feel!"

*****

91

All of the birthday guests were gone, and the house was clean and quiet. Isaiah had put on some slow R&B, dimmed the lights, and grabbed Rebbie's hand. They made slow circles in the middle of the family room, swaying and holding each other close. "I feel good tonight, Baby," Isaiah said.

"You should be feeling good! You on your second bottle of wine," Rebbie said with a laugh.

"You sure?" Isaiah leaned back with a questioning look. "Second bottle… yes!" Rebbie mocked him with a stern look and then laughed again. "I ain't mad at you, Daddy. Raising them boys 21 years… not many Black fathers can say that." She put her head on his shoulder and relaxed into his arms. "Every day is Father's Day around here."

"Sure is, baby." Isaiah felt the warmth of his wife against him and tightened the circle of his arms around her waist. He breathed deeply, "Damn, Baby!"

"What?"

Isaiah massaged Rebbie's back and whispered into her ear, "You looking and smelling good."

"Thank you, Daddy," she said, blushing. "You give me what I need."

"We need to take this upstairs so I can give you another set of twins. Smack another double!" He grinned and smacked her backside.

"I'm always ready for you… but I don't know 'bout them twins, though."

"Okay then, what about triplets?"

The look on Rebbie's face said, 'Yeah… right,' but she gave her husband a seductive smile before grabbing his hand and leading him toward the staircase.

*****

E sat on the passenger side with Angela driving his car. He was blindfolded and holding the dashboard while she drove down what seemed like a very bumpy road. "Damn, girl! Watch the potholes! This gotta be Fulton County!"

"Be quiet, crazy!" Angela laughed and slowly brought the car to a stop. "Anyway, we here so take the rag off your eyes."

E slid the bandana off and looked around, waiting for his eyes to focus. They immediately locked on the large red neon letters of a sign right in front of them. "Obsessions…?! the swingers spot?" He looked at Angela, eyeing her up and down. "Damn girl, you wild!"

"Happy birthday!" she squealed. "Sex is one thing I know you like. So tonight, I want you and me to have another partner." She watched E's eyes grow wider. "Not no ugly chick, though. She gotta be fine like me."

"Having you and another fine ass woman would be the bomb, baby."

"Mmm-hmm…" Angela rolled her eyes. "Just make sure that dick don't be fucking raw tonight."

"Hell nah, baby! You know I'm all about the prophylactics!"

Inside the club, it wasn't long before E and Angela were getting attention from both males and females. Eventually, one female caught both their eyes. The sexy blonde got a hang of their vibe, and moved closer with her eyes glued to E. She stopped in front of Angela and started to kiss her while caressing the front of her body.

"Hell yeah," E said under his breath, getting more and more turned on. Later, inside a private room, he was shirtless with the same blonde bent over in front of him, naked. Angela stood only a few feet away, watching him stroke in and out.

"Look at my birthday boy! Hit that ass, Papi!" Angela said over the loud music playing in the room. "Ooh yeah… beat that pussy!"

"Aaaah… yeah… feels good!" the blonde moaned in pleasure. "Get it…! Go deeper!" E responded by giving her his full length. "Fuck me harder! Harder!" she continued to moan.

"You want it like that, huh?" E smirked and pounded even harder.

"Yes! *Damn…*" she moaned. "Aaaah… shit! That cock is good!"

"Damn right. You like every inch of this dick," E said to the back of her head.

Tired of watching, Angela walked toward them. "E, baby, I want some more of that dick. Fuck me some more," she said, almost begging.

They didn't see the room door open and a black female walk into the room. "Damn, white boy!" She stood staring at the action. "You hittin' it like that? Can I get some? I don't mind you breaking my back."

*****

J and Rachel said goodbye to their friends at the club, and then drove back to his house. In his bedroom, the lights were off and slow music was playing. Rachel straddled his body on the bed, rubbing his chest.

"My man did his thing! Spoke that real talk to the people! Your fan base is growing," she said proudly. "Brothers and sistas screamin' '*J!... J!*' Your name is getting out there."

"Mmm-hmm… like your breasts," he said, smiling in the dark. "Big, brown, soft nipples feeling right. Nice and hard." J shifted beneath Rachel so her full weight was on his midsection. He lifted his head from the bed and their lips met in a long, deep kiss. Then he unhooked her bra and pulled her shirt over her head.

"Ooh!" Rachel squealed and laughed when J flipped her onto her back. She bit her lip, anticipating the feel of him inside of her. Soon he was between her legs, stroking and going deep. "Aaah… Baby! Yes! Ah-ah-ah! Aaah!

95

The next morning, J walked into the kitchen to see Isaiah sitting at the table watching the news on television. He grabbed a plate from the cabinet and heaped it with food Rebbie had left warming on the stove. "Morning, Pop," he said, sitting next to his father.

"Good morning! Feel good to be twenty-one?" Isaiah asked, patting J on the shoulder. "Woke up with a damn appetite, I see," he said, eyeing J's plate. Then, "Tell me something, son," he asked, "when are you gonna follow in your brother's footsteps and get your own place? You can learn a lot from E."

J shrugged without looking up. "I don't know."

"Well, with all this banging headboards, you need your own house. Not no apartment." Isaiah smiled and slapped J's shoulder again, ending with a look that let his son know he actually wasn't joking.

"Oh, I can learn from E, huh?" J sighed and shook his head. "Anyway… I got some spots to check out." He moved the food around his plate and half-listened to the reporter's voice on tv. The only other sound was ice dropping from the automatic maker inside the freezer.

"I hope you know that's your wife," Isaiah said, breaking the silence between them.

J's head jerked to one side, and he looked confused. "Nah, Pop. It's nothing like that. We ain't ready to take that step."

"I was expecting a better answer than that! From what I heard last night, you did a whole lot of penetrating, so that makes her your wife." Isaiah got up to pour another cup of coffee. "Own wife, own house…" he held out one hand and then the other, "the two go together. And… you should have your trust fund money plus prize money."

"Yeah, I'm not doing too bad."

"You shouldn't be! Call it free rent for the past twenty-one years." Isaiah sat back down at the table. "So, you won that money last night?"

"You know I did! I spoke the truth as always… never lies, Pop."

"As you speak it, one must also walk it."

"I do my best. I mean… I keep it humble for the most part," J said with a smile. He stood up from the table.

"How much was the grand prize last night?" Isaiah asked.

"Only five hundred dollars."

Isaiah reached into his pocket and pulled out a money clip full of bills. He counted out one thousand dollars in hundred-dollar bills and slapped it into J's palm. "Here son, here's your five hundred for the work you put in last week. Plus, I'm matching the five hundred you won last night."

J fanned the cash in his hand, then folded it. "Thanks, Pop!"

"It's more about asking the father to remember good deeds. Making sure your good outweighs the bad. Money is just a tool for defense."

"True, 'cause madness is everywhere amongst my generation. And it's spreading with the quickness!" J said, shaking his head. "But hey, I appreciate the five hundred!"

Isaiah looked up at a clock on the wall and grabbed his keys and phone from the kitchen counter. J glanced at the time on his phone and realized it was time for his father to leave for work. "Just remember our conversation, son. And if you see your brother, tell him to stop by the office."

"I'll go see him before I come in. Is Kenya gonna be there?"

"Yeah, she's supposed to be in at one o'clock. Me, Joe, and Carlos got people to hunt down."

"Alright, be safe, Pop."

"I will. Talk to you later. And get that message to your brother."

Chapter Nine

Roxy had the volume turned down on the tv in E and Angela's front room. She leaned against one corner of the couch with her legs tucked beneath her, watching music videos and singing along to herself. Outside, a car door closed, and she heard footsteps approaching the front door. She jumped up to see who was outside, even before the heavy knock. She was excited to see J standing on the other side of the door. Come on in, J!"

"What's up, lil chica!" J reached for a quick hug. "Is he up?"

"Let me go check." Roxy turned and headed upstairs.

J stood with his arms crossed for a second, and then headed for the couch. That's when he saw cases of liquor stacked and lining the walls. "Damn bruh," he muttered under his breath, "I see what you did with your trust fund money!"

"He'll be down in a minute." Roxy came and plopped back down on the opposite end of the couch.

"You okay, little girl?" he asked.

"I'm fine now," she answered with a sweet smile.

"Oh, okay," he said, grinning. Then, changing the subject, "You sleep good?"

"After the party, I just stayed up messing around on the chat line. But I'm cool."

"You just turned fifteen, right?" J asked, sizing her up. "My birthday is May 29th. Gemini, just like you."

"No doubt. We at the top of the chain," he said.

"Us Gemini's know how to keep it real, no matter what." Roxy looked J up and down. She licked her lips, and let her eyes rest on his mouth. "Damn, Rachel is lucky." She was enjoying the uncomfortable look on his face and smiled when he opened his mouth to reply. But before any more words passed between them, E came jogging down the stairs.

"What's going on, bruh?" he asked, giving J dap. "What's good?"

Roxy sat there, and E noticed her still staring and lusting over J. "Roxy, your business is upstairs. Grown men talking!" E said, nodding toward the stairs.

Roxy took her eyes off J long enough to roll them at E. "Just 'cause you twenty-one now don't mean you can boss me." She stood from the couch and turned to leave the room. "Bye, J!"

"Later, Roxy." J shook his head at the floor and laughed. "Boy… she just like Angela. Love running that mouthpiece."

"What time you get in?" J asked, changing the subject. "Shit… after eight this morning. Stopped by Waffle House and threw down like three plates of waffles."

"Damn, boy! You had the munchkins!" J said, laughing. Hell yeah! And it wasn't from no weed." E clapped his hands and rubbed them together. "Bet my birthday present was better than yours!"

"Mine was good," J said. "That Moscato had me right. But…" he pointed to the cases of liquor against the walls, "I see the party ain't over."

E looked to where his brother was pointing and shook his head. "Not mine. Angela's uncle asked me would I keep it over here 'til Friday. Muthafucker throwing a weekend party. Scared he might drink that shit up!"

"Word? Unc be drinking like a fish?"

"All day, every day."

"*Daaamn*!" J burst out laughing.

"I told Angela that wino can't come over here no more."

"Word."

But yo, man… ooh wee!" E covered his mouth with his fist and laughed.

"What?" J had a puzzled look.

"I was smashing two to three bitches at a time last night!"

"Oh shit! You had that ménage going on?"

"Hell yeah! At the swingers club," E boasted. "Wait… where the hell was Angela?"

"Getting served, too." E's ego swelled when J's eyes stretched wide. "Had my bottom bitch right beside me."

"A bunch of freaks, you and Angela," J said, shaking his head.

"Don't hate! Angela wanted to make a movie. My girl showed me a good time."

"Hate on a bunch of fornicators?" J waved his hands in a slicing motion in front of his throat. "Never that."

"Anyway, man!" E sucked his teeth and jokingly rolled his eyes at his brother. Changing the subject, he said, "I know you rocked the mic at the club."

J leaned back against the couch with a proud smile on his face. "You know I did! Same results as always. First prize winner!" he said and snapped his collar.

"Hell yeah!" E reached over and slapped five with his brother. "We need to put out a CD. Let these fools hear something real."

"Maybe one day soon." J nodded in agreement. Then he started to look around the room and peered past E toward the kitchen. "Say man, how much is this spot running you?"

"Twelve hundred a month," E said. "Why? Pop kicking you out?" He picked up the remote and started flipping through channels on tv.

"Sort of," J said, clearly sounding like he had an attitude.

"Fuck outta here!" E said from the opposite end of the couch. "Pops and Mom want they shit to themselves. That's why I made my move early."

"Ha!" J laughed. "That's bullshit. You like bein' in the streets. *That's* why you moved."

"Man, shut up!" E threw a fake punch in J's direction.

"*You* shut up… popping that dumb shit. Anyway man, Pop said for you to stop by the office."

"For what?" E asked.

"What you think? Locating them violators. Time to put some work in." J watched his brother's expression turn sour. "What?"

E shook his head slowly. "I can't be sitting behind no desk talkin' on the phone. That ain't enough action for me."

"Well, you know Pop want us to learn the business side first. The paperwork and other important matters."

"And we can't be bounty hunters 'til what age, bruh?"

"Twenty-five." J rested his elbows on his knees and dropped his head, anticipating E's reaction.

"Four more years?! *Maaan…* I'm getting paper *now*, J! Now ain't the time to hesitate." E stood from the couch. "Remember that one time we were hunting, and you had a buck in your sights? But you hesitated and missed the shot?"

J remembered that day all too well. "Yeah, I remember."

"I can't nut up right now, lil bruh."

"Man, I get it. Get your paper. Just try and avoid all that illegal stuff. Don't let all that shit cloud your mind."

"Nah J, Angela looking into opening a massage spa. So moves gotta be made, feel me?" He stared absently at the tv for a few seconds, and then stuffed a hand into one of his front pockets. "How much was the prize money last night?"

"Five hundred, why?" J watched E pull out a wad of cash and count out five bills.

"Take this." E reached out to hand J the money, but was confused by the look on his brother's face.

"Hell you doing?" J asked. "I got money."

"Relax, J. I know you still sitting on your trust fund." E nudged the bills against J's hand until he opened his fingers and took them. "It's towards your move. Get a nice crib for you and Rachel."

"Good looking out, bruh."

"Yeah," E said, nodding his head toward the front door. "Right 'round the corner they got some nice condos."

"I thought you spent all your trust fund money on parties," J said jokingly.

"Hell nah, lil bruh! I flipped my twenty-five thousand already… ten times over," E said proudly with his chin up.

"So that mean you are not trying to learn the family business?"

"Not right now. I gotta do me, bruh."

"That's what's up then," J said. "Give Pop a call and let him know what's going on."

"For sho! Don't worry 'bout me, lil bruh. I'll give Pop a jingle later on."

*****

Walking through the house, E could hear Angela and her sister Roxy in the bedroom cursing loudly in Spanish. He knew enough to know they were calling somebody a dirty bitch, and the two of them were figuring out what to do about a situation. "Puta Sucio!" Angela screamed.

104

"Si! Si!" Roxy agreed. "Que vamos a hacer?"

E walked into the room and stood for a few seconds, listening and shaking his head before cutting in. "Whenever y'all in here going off in Spanish, it's always some shit."

"We got another pervert sweating Roxy," Angela said. "Who?" E asked.

Angela jumped out of her seat and strutted in a circle with her chest poked out. "I said *Jeeesus!* Yes, *Jeeesus!* Jesus *died* for your sins! Can I get a amen?" she dramatized with a crooked grin.

"Who… Eddie Long?" he asked.

"No, Eddie like lil boys," Angela said, rolling her eyes. "I'm talking 'bout Pastor Wallace, fool!" Angela laughed when she saw that E was at a loss for words. "Roxy, I told you. Look at him. Shit caught him off guard."

"You fucking kidding me." E turned to Roxy. "That fool came at you?"

"Yep. Sure did," Roxy answered. "For real… no bullshit."

"No lie. I'm keeping it real."

"I *know* Pop couldn't been around when he made his move."

"Uh-uh… your dad was inside the house when he was asking for my name and number."

E gave Roxy a puzzled look. "Say what? Did you tell him your age?"

"Told him with the quickness," Roxy said, raising an eyebrow and crossing her arms.

"And that porkchop-eating muthafucker was *still* lusting?!" E looked at Roxy and then to Angela, who just nodded in agreement. "So, did you give up some info? Your phone number?"

Roxy shrugged. "I told him that it come with a price tag. Just to see what he say. And he said it wasn't a problem."

"That moreno got big balls, with his wife in the *same house!*" Angela chimed in.

E walked across the room and looked out the front window. "OG said money ain't a problem, huh? It's like *that* Mister Pastor Man?" He turned and asked Roxy, "He got your number?"

"She gave him mine," Angela said. She looked at E's back, wondering what was going through his mind.

"All them years, he came around flexing like he's a man of God. If my Pops knew this man like popping underage pussy, Pastor Wallace would be a *dead* man."

"He ain't no fucking man... *low life fucker*," Angela said, sucking her teeth.

"Perverted son of a bitch, that's what he is. But..." E turned from the window to look at them both, "... I know one way to inflict pain.

"You not gonna shoot him, are you?" Roxy asked nervously.

"Nah, lil chica. That slick talker is better alive. Hit him where it hurts."

"Hit him where?" Roxy asked, confused.

"That fucker got big cheese, Roxy." E pointed to Angela. "Big Sis gonna tell you how to get it." Angela nodded.

*****

Isaiah, Joe, and another of Isaiah's employees, Carlos sat parked on the street inside of a black SUV. They had been there for almost three hours, staking out the known residence of a suspect. As the hours dragged on, Carlos helped pass the time by cracking jokes and kidding his boss about the empty fast food containers and coffee cups that littered the floor and dashboard of the vehicle. But when a white, late model Camaro passed them and then pulled into a nearby driveway, the three men stopped talking and focused their attention on the car. The streetlights gave a clear view of the two people inside – the suspect Jeff Moore and his girlfriend, who was behind the wheel. "Looks like our car," Carlos said. "White Camaro with dark tint."

"Uh-huh…" Joe said slowly, "but let's wait 'til he gets out."

Inside the Camaro, Jeff turned to look at his girlfriend. She hadn't talked much the whole ride over. "So, how long are you gonna be?" he asked.

"Not long. My sister asked me to take her to the store."

"Don't be all damn day!" he showed her a mean mug and then laughed.

"Don't worry, I'm not," she said. "Shit… I'm too damn hungry. So what's for dinner?"

107

"I don't know. Pick something up on the way back. Oh, and a carton of Camels."

"Okay, baby," she said, leaning over to give him a peck on the lips. "Let me go so I can hurry back."

"Alright… and tell your sister to give you some gas money. Fuck that!" Jeff lifted the door handle and stepped out of the car.

"Okay Joe, let's move!" Isaiah said as soon as Jeff's feet were on the ground. They crept toward their suspect, closing in quickly.

Walking towards the house, Jeff reached into his front pockets and realized he left his phone inside the car. In a few steps, he was back at the passenger side door, but it was locked. He bumped the window with his fist. "Open the door. I forgot my phone." When the lock didn't click open, he leaned down to look at his girlfriend's face, but he could tell her eyes were fixed on something behind him.

"Jeff Moore, we have a warrant for your arrest," Isaiah said in a loud, steady tone.

"Let's see your hands!" Joe yelled.

"Bitch, open the fucking door!" Jeff hit the window harder with his fist. Looking into her eyes, he suddenly realized the truth of what was happening. "You set me up!" It almost came out as a question. "Goddammit bitch, I'll kill you!"

She screamed back at him through tears that were streaming down her face. "No! Fuck you! I don't want this no more! I'm tired of the damn beatings!" For a second, Jeff was stunned by her words and by the anguished look on her face. He pulled up on the door handle again, and leaned his forehead against the window when it didn't open. Joe and Isaiah both pulled their weapons and pointed them at his back.

"Let me see your hands! Hands!" Joe shouted again. Carlos pulled up in the truck to block any path of escape. Isaiah rushed in to grab Jeff's arms and put cuffs on him.

"Get the fuck off me, dude! You twisting my arm!" Jeff yelled while squirming in pain.

"Calm your damn nerves and settle your ass down! The ducking and hiding is over for you!" Isaiah jerked on the cuffs behind Jeff's back. "And no more being a tough guy on your woman."

"Fuck you saying, man? Jesus Christ!" Jeff protested.

"No more knocking out womens' teeth is what I'm saying."

"Wait… what the hell is going on? That ain't me! Who teeth I knocked out, sir?" Jeff strained to try and look at Isaiah.

"Enough with the games, woman beater. I love locking up cowards like you."

"Let me explain, sir!"

"Too late for that. You missed that court date, so now you get to be a tough guy in a 6 x 9."

Joe laughed and mocked Jeff's pleading, "*Let go! Let me explain!* Yeah… that's what cowards always say. I got a seat for you, jackass!"

Jeff's girlfriend watched from inside her car but got out as soon as she saw that Jeff was restrained. "You happy now bitch?! You set me up!" Jeff hollered. "I'll see you again, you cunt!"

Joe opened a backdoor to their vehicle and held it wide as Isaiah stuffed Jeff inside. His girlfriend gave him a steely glare and raised her middle finger. "Fuck you."

*****

E and one of his soldiers, Benjamin, sat in a car parked to one side of the lot in front of a convenience store. They sat in silence, watching the activity in front of the building. After a while, E opened his door and got out, with Benjamin following his lead.

Walking towards the store, he caught the eye of his guy Antonio, who immediately moved in his direction.

"Everything on point?" E asked. "Walk with me." They walked off into the shadows to talk in private, leaving Benjamin on post in front of the entrance.

"Shit been busy. Muthafuckers dropping their *whole check* on the slots." Antonio grinned and shook his head.

"Any new faces?" E asked. "Nah."

"Alright, cool. But hey, Grandma Doli been texting me back-to-back. She need them cases of liquor ASAP."

"Maaan…" Antonio rubbed his hands together and shook his head.

"What?" E asked, waiting to hear whatever Antonio was holding back.

110

"Uncle Thomas still causing problems. Eddie almost shot him."

"What you mean, *almost shot him*? What the fuck going on?"

"Man, that nigga still stealing liquor and fucking up house money! After plenty warnings. So Grandma confronted him… and the nigga was bold enough to laugh in her face!"

E's anger was rising. "For real? Laughed in her face, huh?"

"Yeah!" Antonio became more and more animated. "But you know Eddie wasn't having it, folk. Grandma ended up pleading with that nigga not to kill his uncle."

"Why the fuck I'm just finding out 'bout this madness?"
"Didn't wanna fuck up your birthday, E," Antonio answered apologetically.

E looked at the ground and sucked his teeth. "Who at the register?"

"Cousin Anna."

"I'm gonna go in here and make this pick up real quick. Take Mackie with you over to that nigga's crib. Wait all night if you have to. I want his ass dead. Feel me?"

"Bet."

"Post up. I'll be back in a minute." E walked away from Antonio and signaled Benjamin to follow. Inside the store was the regular scene. The front was bright with fluorescent lights, with Anna and the owner behind the counter. Past the coolers and racks of snacks and groceries, the back of the room was darker with just the flashing multicolored lights of slot machines.

Almost every machine had somebody standing or sitting in front of it.

Anna saw E walk through the door and waved to him. "Hey, E!"

"What's good, baby?"

"Everything!"

"Yo-Yo! Sareed, everything good?" E called to the store owner.

Sareed looked away from a customer and gave E a thumbs up. "One minute, big man." He finished with the customer and then walked over to unlock and open a door marked 'OFFICE'.

"Holla at me!" Anna yelled to E.

"No doubt. Real soon, baby." E, Benjamin, and Sareed walked into the office, and there was a loud click as the door closed and locked behind them. Sareed walked directly to a desk on the opposite wall and opened a drawer.

"Here, bro. I got it for you."

"Dis eighty thousan' dollar, mon?" Benjamin locked his eyes on Sareed with a hard stare.

"Yeah, brother. I don't come short with y'all."

Benjamin sucked his teeth. "Me pray ya come two dolla short so me can take ya life." Sareed shrugged in confusion and looked back and forth between Benjamin and E.

"He ain't your damn brother," E said, his voice filling the small room. "That's what sand niggas tell bruhs makin' sistas feel comfortable." E took an envelope from Sareed's hand and began fanning through the bills inside. "Yeah, you a wild man... give a sista a six-pack for a blow job." He knew the store owner was scared and didn't know what might happen next, and that made him smile. "Don't ever short me. And never think you can always stick your dick where you please."

Once they were back inside the car, E asked Benjamin, "Man, how you like this M45?"

"Dis bad boi is right! 350 horses. Dis muthafucka buck mon!"

"Yeah... like Uncle Thomas, bucking too many times," E said. He looked at his watch and then glanced around the outside of the car, "Time to put that batty asshole to rest, eh?"

"I got rules to this shit." E opened the door to spit on the ground and then quickly pulled it shut. "Disrespecting Grandma... stealing, and then *laughing* in her face? Shit like that piss me off. Who the fuck he think he playing with?"

Benjamin stroked his chin and nodded. "So... who blasting that bumbaclot?"

"Antonio and Mackie got the order. Shit... Mackie *been* wanting to do him," E said with a laugh. "But for real though... once Grandma hear about the murder, it might devastate her and Eddie. So giving them support is a top priority. Feel me?"

"No doubt. Whatever yah say."

Chapter Ten

Isaiah and Rebbie's family room was empty except for J laid out on the couch asleep. Scenes from days gone by and the voices of E and his father filled his dreams. *'Good shot! Now that's my boy right there! That's how you do it!'* His mind played back the proud look on Isaiah's face when E killed the huge buck. *'When will you follow in E's footsteps?*

Follow in E's footsteps... You know that's your wife, right? Your wife, right... Knocking headboards... You need your own place... Tell your brother to come see me... You could learn something from E... That's my boy right there!' Over and over, the words echoed in J's mind.

Rebbie walked into the dark room and could barely make out the outline of J's body on the couch. She turned on a lamp and moved closer. He was mumbling and moving his head from side to side. "J... J!" She shook his shoulder to wake him from the dream.

"Huh?" J woke suddenly and practically jumped off the couch. He blinked his eyes and tried to focus on Rebbie's face. She was standing over him with her hands on her hips.

"J... J! You talk to E?" She watched him nod yes, and then walked away. "Hmph! I be telling Isaiah that boy is in his own world," she said under her breath. J sat up and watched his mother leave the room, still trying to shake the cobwebs from his brain and return to reality from his dream.

Inside The Spot seemed muggy compared to the cool night air outside. E walked around the inside perimeter of the small warehouse building. The crowd inside was drinking, listening to music, and playing slots and pool. He laid eyes on his grandmother, Doli, and gave her a hug. She returned the hug with a tight squeeze.

"Hey, my Hatki son," she said, calling him *my white son* in her Native American language. She gently patted E's cheek. "Everything good with you?"

"Everything is blessed, Grandma. We good here." "And we straight over here. Eddie ain't having no mess from *nobody* – don't matter *who* it is. He say, '*Momma, ain't nobody fucking up what E do for us*'."

"Where is Eddie?" E asked, looking around the room.

Suddenly Grandma's expression changed. "Don't get mad," she said nervously.

"Nah, you know better than that, Grandma. I can't get mad at you."

"I sent him to the liquor store."

E looked puzzled and pointed over his shoulder toward the entrance. "I got all the texts. We brought a trunk full... Ben bringing that shit in now."

"I didn't know what time you was coming through, and I *need* that liquor. Besides, he just picking up some strong drink for

Thomas and his friends."

A few miles away, Mackie and Antonio had Uncle Thomas in their sights. They sat inside Mackie's car watching him handle a transaction from the trunk of his own vehicle. "We got that wanna-be chief. Selling Grandma shit for the low. Give me the okay so I can make his heart stop cuz," Mackie sneered.

Antonio held his hand up. "Hold up, bruh. Let him do his thing… make that money for us." They watched Uncle Thomas and the buyer finish up, and the associate walk back to his truck. As the other man pulled off, Thomas closed his trunk and started to get in his car. But, looking like he forgot something, he went back to the trunk and opened it again. "Let's do this." Antonio said calmly, tying a bandana to cover the lower part of this face. Mackie slowly pulled up behind Uncle Thomas' car. Antonio got out, silently approaching Thomas from behind.

"Hey, Tonto! Where my drink?" Mackie yelled from the driver's side window.

Startled, Uncle Thomas jerked around. "Who the fuck is you?" he said, trying to shield his eyes from the headlights.

"The Lone Ranger, muthafucker!"

Thomas never even saw Antonio walk up behind him. *Pop! Pop! Pop!* His body fell over into the trunk of the car. Mackie hopped out and walked over. He reached past the body to grab the remaining cases of liquor from the trunk. "Give me this shit!

Robbing from the family. You wanna be chief, huh?"

Back at The Spot, Eddie had returned from his liquor run and was behind the bar making drinks for E and Benjamin and two women sitting with them. "Here you go, sweetheart," he said, sliding a glass to the female sitting at E's side.

"Mmm... that's good," she said after taking a sip. "Thank you! I might need another one later on."

"You got it! No problem."

The woman touched E on the shoulder and said, "Talk to you later." E nodded as she walked away.

E leaned toward Eddie so he didn't have to shout over the loud music. "I heard you were about to burn somebody."

"It came close to that. Real fucking close. But everything's good."

"Can't see Grandma taking no losses, feel me?" "Course not, E. Believe me, we got everything straight,"

Eddie assured him.

"No larceny shit?"

Before Eddie could answer, Honey, a regular at The Spot, walked to the bar and stood beside E. "I need a drink, Mr. Bartender."

"Sure, what can I get you?" Eddie asked. "Can you make me a Blue Motherfucker?"

Eddie nodded. "I got you, sweetheart."

Honey looked at E and sighed, "It ain't fun losing. 'Specially when you gamble with your rent money."

E shook his head. "How much you lose on the pool table?" "Just fifty dollars," she said. "And *that* unattractive muthafucker beat me." She nodded in the direction of an older guy standing near the tables. When E looked over, he saw the man already staring back at him.

"His eyes were on my ass the whole time! Made me uncomfortable," she said with a shiver.

Just then, E's phone rang. It was Antonio. "Hold that thought, baby." He turned to the side and held a finger over one ear to block the noise from the room. "Hello!"

"That's taken care of."

"Sounds good. Talk to you later." E ended the call and turned back to the woman at the bar. "What's your name? Chocolate?"

She laughed and answered, "Nah baby, it's Honey. What's yours?" E saw that her eyes rested on something behind him. He turned to see the same dude from the pool tables now standing right in front of him.

"What's up, Esau?"

"Who you calling Esau?" E asked with a smirk. "Do I look like my name some muthafucking Esau to you?"

"You the only cracker sitting at the bar!"

E stood up and leaned in like he was hard of hearing. "What did you just call me?

"What, you can't hear...? cracker?" The man puffed out his

chest. "You heard what I called you."

Benjamin stopped talking to the woman beside him at the bar. "Excuse me for a minute," he said politely. He rose and stood beside E.

"I got this Ben," E said. Ben put his hands up and started to back away.

Then, *Wham*! E landed a punch to the side of the man's face, then grabbed his throat and forced him to the floor. "Speak now! Say it! Say it, muthafucker! I can't hear you! I'm gonna shut your mouth for good, bitch!" E pulled a knife from his ankle holster and drew his hand back. But Ben moved in and grabbed E's arm to keep him from swinging the blade.

"Easy nuh, mon… easy. Get off him." Ben pried the knife from E's clenched fingers. "Don't do it. Come on," he said, "this ain't the place to kill 'im. Too many witnesses to deal wit'. *Think*!" He grabbed E's shoulder and shook him.

"That's what I *wanna* do… kill this bastard!" E's eyes were on fire and his chest heaved in anger, but he allowed Benjamin to pull him off the man. He got to his feet and sneered, "Watch who you call a cracker, bitch!" Walking back to the bar he nodded to Eddie. "Throw this garbage outta here!" He looked around at the crowd that stood by, gawking in silence. "Anybody got something to say? You can get some, too."

Eddie came from behind the bar and grabbed the man by the collar. "Come on, get up! Let's go, man… leaking blood on the damn floor. Your shit-talking days are over, buddy!"

With the fight over and things calmed down, everyone went back to what they were doing before, enjoying the night. But suddenly, hysterical screams were coming from the back of the building.

Grandma Doli appeared in the middle of the crowd with tears in her eyes, calling for Eddie. "No, Great Spirit! No! Can't be!" She rushed across the floor, yelling and shaking her hands. "Oh no… don't tell me that! Eddie! Eddie!"

"What? What is it? What now?" Eddie was just walking back through the door from outside.

"Thomas is dead!" she sobbed. "He got robbed and shot in front of his house!" She collapsed against Eddie as soon as he reached for her.

*****

Isaiah was at his desk sifting through a stack of papers and discussing cases with Kenya when E and J walked in. "Where you been?" he asked E right away.

"What you mean, Pop?"

"What the hell you think I mean?" Isaiah let the papers fall from his hands onto the desk with a loud thud. J and Kenya exchanged uneasy looks. "You stopped coming to work," Isaiah said matter-of-factly. "I call your phone, left messages, but don't get a return call."

"Calm down, Pop. It's not like that," E said, trying to ease the tension in the room.

"I don't care who hears me! Everybody in here got damn problems... some hard-headed loved one, or a ignorant damn family member. You better start living according to what I taught you!" Isaiah snarled.

"I don't forget nothing. My life is good Pop," E said and shrugged nonchalantly. "I'm staying outta trouble. Me and Angela got this opportunity to open a body massage and spa business."

"Do you know what the hell you doing? Do You?

What... you got some girls ready to serve some old Chinese guys when their dicks get hard?"

"Nah, Pop. No prostitution. Strictly legal. Everything legit. We got certified workers."

"So what... Jones Bail Bond ain't qualified enough?" "Ah man, listen to yourself, Pop!"

Isaiah leaned forward with one eyebrow raised, pointing a finger at E. "You better watch your words. I'm not your *man*. I'm your father."

"Sorry Pop, but I'm just trying to get mine the same way you got yours."

Isaiah sat back slowly with a smirk on his face. "Don't fool with me, son. I ain't new to the game. Have you forgotten what we do here?" he said, waving his hand around the office. "What type of people you think I bond out? Those businesses bring in all types of shit. And not one time have you mentioned the Father. I got mine with the help of *him*, not no woman."

"Things changed, Pop. We helping *each other*. That's the way it is these days."

"Son, I knew what you went through with all the name-calling and finger-pointing from kids *and* adults. So if you feel like you doing this to prove a point, ain't no need. I'm a hard-working Black man that has twin sons – one white, the other Black. A big challenge was given to me and I couldn't fail. I love you and wasn't afraid to show it or say it. Whoever finds fault is my enemy… as well as God."

"And I understand all that," E said, "because I accepted my skin color. And if other people didn't, so be it. See Pop, I work to be rich one day, not middle class. I want it all."

Isaiah threw his hands up. "So it's about money?! The pimps, thugs and drug dealers want it all, too! Nice cars, big houses, and women with big butts!"

"Nah, Pop! Man, it ain't like that." "Didn't I just tell you I'm not your man?" "Sorry! I don't mean nothing by it, but…"

Isaiah cut E off from speaking. "I offer you a company that I built for thirty years, and you say *no*?" The room was quiet for a few seconds. Then Isaiah yelled suddenly, "Get the hell outta my office!"

"It's like that, Pop...? Okay." E was visibly shaken. He turned and rushed out of the office, pushing past J and Kenya.

"Yo, E! What's up?" J called behind his brother. E didn't

answer, and then the outside door swung open and slammed shut. J hurried outside and looked up and down the street in both directions. He saw E walking at a fast pace down the block and pulled out his phone to call him.

E answered on the first ring. "What up, lil bruh?"

"What's the deal, storming out like you on a mission?" "Pop be on that old school shit too hard."

J could see that E had stopped walking and was standing in the middle of the sidewalk at the end of the block. "That old school way protected your ass growing up." He and E were now facing each other. "So… you told Pop about your business?"

"You know I did. Times changed, J. Money is everywhere. It's all about getting your own, no matter what. I'm fucking *proud* of what I do!"

"Bullshit!"

"Fuck you saying? I'm full of shit 'cause I like giving orders the same as Pop?"

"Man, your money-making schemes got your mind twisted. Get your shit together, big bruh… before you lose what's more important."

E raised his fist and middle finger high so J could see it. "Fuck your advice, J! Who the fuck named you Job? Like you keeping shit upright!"

"Stay stuck on stupid and watch who get played at the end!" J heard the line go dead, and down the street, he could see E walking backwards, still looking in J's direction with his middle finger in the air.

Back inside the building, Kenya poked her head inside the door to Isaiah's office. "Knock-knock."

"Yeah."

"Just a little reminder about me taking this Monday and Tuesday off," she said, walking into the room. "I got an appointment at the beach and I can't be late."

"My son walk in here and tell me where I can put my business, and now one of my best agents is taking time off 'cause she got an appointment with vitamin D."

"Hmph! Isaiah…" Kenya whined.

"I didn't forget!" Isaiah chuckled, waving his hand. "You just like a family member… looking for days off.

*****

Angela sat at a computer desk in her and E's spare bedroom with him looking over her shoulder. The monitor showed a security camera feed from different rooms in the house. "Bam! Clear shot. We got all the angles covered for that fucking weirdo." One of the frames showed Roxy walking through the living room.

"It's recording Roxy right now? Live?" E asked.

"Everything, baby. Got that Scarface shit on him. The technician hooked us up! Camera one shows the front door and the living room."

"What about Roxy's room?"

"Hell no! No need for that. That worm-faced fucker ain't getting that far. You taught me the element of surprise. Fucks 'em up every time! We got that puta in a trap."

E gripped her shoulders and started massaging them. "Giving surprises is your specialty," he said, giving her a quick kiss on the neck.

"I play my position big time. Now close your eyes... 'cause it's time for you to feed your baby." Angela started to make sounds like a baby crying. "Waaah... Waaah..." She undid E's pants and put his rigid penis into her mouth.

"Shit... it's feeding time. Do your thing, girl." E grinned and watched the back and forth motion of Angela's head.

*****

J held the small plastic basket and walked beside Rachel as she looked for items in the grocery store. She put a small package into the basket and then reached for his other hand. "E came by today to holla at Pop," he said.

"Oh yeah? How did it go?"

"Not too good. E let him know he didn't wanna work in the family business."

Rachel looked surprised. "For real?"

"Yeah, and Pops lost it! Told him to get the hell out." They stopped in the middle of the aisle.

"Whoa! No, Pops didn't!" Rachel tried not to laugh. "Yeah, Pop was lighting his ass up, baby!"

Rachel squeezed J's hand and asked him, "How do you feel about it?".

"I ain't stressing nothing"

"I know you handle yours, baby. And do a good job at it, too." Rachel took another couple of steps, and then stopped in her tracks. "Hold on. Is that… *Darius*?" She tugged at J's arm to get his attention.

"Where?"

Down the aisle, Rachel saw two familiar faces. From a distance, she could swear it was Darius, holding his grandmother's hand. "Down the aisle to your right." Rachel nodded in their direction.

J looked dumbfounded. "Hold on, baby. This shit makes no sense," he said under his breath. Together he and Rachel walked slowly to the other end of the aisle. Getting closer, they clearly saw it *was* Darius standing with his grandmother. But something was off. Darius was staring at the floor and swaying from side to side. The elderly woman looked over to them and smiled.

Rachel smiled and waved to her. "Hey, Darius," she said. But instead of responding, Darius kept his eyes on the floor with his head nodding repeatedly.

"How y'all doing?" the grandmother asked.

"We're fine. How are you doing?" J reached out and patted her shoulder.

"Things are fine now." She looked at her grandson. "Darius is getting a little better. He still have a hard time remembering. Ever since he got in trouble back at that school." She gave J and Rachel a sorrowful look. "Doctors say somebody gave him some bad drugs. Messed up his mind."

Rachel placed a hand over her mouth. Seeing Darius after so long, and in that condition was a real shock. "I didn't know Darius was doing drugs," she said. "That's why we ain't seen him at school? I just thought he transferred to go someplace else."

"No," the grandmother said and shook her head, "after all that happened he couldn't function right, so I had to take him out. Him being a young Black man in America is hard enough. And now *this*… a mental disorder?" She looked back and forth between Rachel and J. But all they could offer were sympathetic stares.

"We're sorry to hear that," J said. He reached out to touch her shoulder again. He could feel a slight tug on his other arm from Rachel, letting him know she was ready to move on.

"We wish you all the best," Rachel said sincerely. "Bye, Darius." She hoped to see a smile or wave. Something that resembled her old schoolmate. But Darius barely moved his eyes to follow her and J as they walked past. "That is so sad," she said once they were out of earshot. "Didn't he used to hang with E and Rock?"

J nodded. "Back in the day when we were younger."

"People do some evil things," Rachel said, sucking her teeth. "I'm so ready for a change of scenery!"

"Me too, baby. I pray for that every day."

Chapter Eleven

Pastor Wallace had made himself comfortable on the sofa in E and Angela's front room. He turned to Roxy, who was sitting at the other end, and said, "So, tell Pastor what you know about the Bible."

"Well… not a lot," Roxy answered with a shrug. "People say Jesus love us all and he died for our sins, right?"

The pastor leaned towards her. "What you *should* know is God has big plans that require you to seek security from a man." He studied the girl's face to see what impact his words were making.

"*Dios mio!*" Roxy made the form of a cross over her chest.

"What was that you said?"

"I said, *Oh my God*. It's hard to come across a guy my age that keeps it real. Most of 'em are immature and liars."

"Yes, you're right." He leaned back, satisfied to be getting a reaction. "Sad but true for most young guys. So… I assume you don't have a man in your life?"

"It's just not for me," Roxy answered.

The pastor grinned. He had brought a Bible with him and sat it between them on the couch. Now he placed his hand on it and slid it toward Roxy. "Turn to Colossians, chapter three, verse one." While she found the page number and then flipped to the passage, he traced the curves of her young body with his eyes. When she finally looked up, their eyes met. "The Bible must be read here a little and there a little. This scripture is one example." He took the Bible from Roxy's hands and read the passage out loud. "Wives submit to your own husband as is fitting in the Lord." Closing the book, he looked at her and said, "A short passage that shows women their place within the relationship."

"So… it's all about the *woman* totally submitting?" Roxy stretched her eyes in disbelief. "Wow, I don't know about that. That's a big shock."

"The Lord also deals with abundance," he said in a low, even tone. "Things that are big…" he paused until she looked at him, "… and penetrate your soul in a deep way."

He felt more and more comfortable and bolder with his choice of words, unaware that his every move was being watched and recorded from another room.

"I bet he talking 'bout his *dick*," Angela said in disgust. She and E were watching a live feed of Roxy and the pastor on a monitor in their bedroom.

"Be quiet! How you know?" E nudged her elbow. They both laughed a little and watched as the pastor placed the Bible to one side and moved closer to Roxy on the couch.

"I don't have a husband, so all that submitting stuff wouldn't apply to me," Roxy said.

"Well, you know… sex constitutes marriage in the sight of God. But since you have no man, there's no adultery." He moved even closer. "When I saw you, I wanted some of you right there."

"Wait... you wanna have sex with me and make me your wife, when you already *have* a wife. A white one at that." Roxy scooted away from him and folded her arms across her chest. "*And...* I'm just fifteen. Ain't that a crime?" Looking at the pastor, she was surprised that her words didn't seem to discourage him at all.

"Only if you tell," he said with a devilish grin. "This is why you can't tell anybody." His eyes ran greedily over her body. "I can be that daddy for you, little mommy. How do you say *pretty* in Spanish?"

"Bonita."

"Roxy is *bonita*. Umph! Yes Lord, very pretty. See how you taught me something?"

"No lie? I just taught you something?"

"Yes, baby." Pastor Wallace slid across the couch cushions and quickly closed the distance between them. He grabbed one of Roxy's hands. "Now... this is much better."

Still watching on video, E stood up. He pulled a gun from his waistband and chambered a round. Angela stood beside him with her eyes fixed on the screen. "Won't be long now before them hands start doing dirty shit," she said.

"That's what we want. Let him make his move. Just keep recording, and when I call you to bring the copy, have it ready," E said. He started to move slowly toward the door. The video feed showed Pastor Wallace moving even closer to Roxy. She didn't move away but was noticeably nervous and fumbled with her hands.

"It's your young smile that's got me wanting you," the pastor said, pointing a finger at Roxy's lips.

"Really?"

"You know what to do." The pastor startled Roxy by reaching out to stroke her neck.

Still watching from the other room, Angela stood up and began pacing the floor. She pointed at the screen. "Look! He's touching her. Go, baby!"

"No, wait! Give him time to really act up." E's eyes were glued to the monitor. He and Angela saw the man slide his hand down from Roxy's neck to her shoulder, and then circle his arm around her shoulders.

"So, you feel like you can touch me?" Roxy said, trying not to sound as nervous as she was.

"I don't see anything wrong with it," he said, drawing her closer. "I can give you something big to rub."

"And what is that?" Roxy said, leaning away as much as she could.

Pastor Wallace stood suddenly, turned towards Roxy, and unzipped his pants. "This big rod between my legs… it needs some attention, too." She sat frozen in disbelief as he took steps in her direction.

"My God!" she gasped, trying to scramble to her feet. But before she could stand, the older man grabbed her arm and held her down. "Please, no! Stop!" Roxy strained against him, trying to twist her wrist out of his grasp.

E and Angela were both frozen in front of the security monitor with their mouths open. Neither could believe what they were actually seeing. "Please go and get him now, baby. Now!" Angela screamed.

"That's enough! That fucking piece of shit!" E rushed from the bedroom with the loaded gun in his hand. By the time he reached the living room, Roxy had been forced onto her back with the pastor on top of her. E could hear her muffled screams as she tried to push him off.

"You know you want this beast inside of you! I won't hurt you, Roxy." The pastor sounded out of breath as he rolled his body on top of her. It was the feeling of cold metal at the back of his head that made him stop suddenly and take his hands off of her.

"What the hell are you doing?! Get off her, pastor man!" E nudged the end of the pistol against the man's skin. "Put your dick away and zip your pants up, muthafucker!"

"Wait… wait now. Ease up!" The pastor's hands shot up in the air, and he rolled away from Roxy and fell onto the floor. "It's not what you think!" he pleaded.

Roxy gathered herself and scrambled off the couch. She ran and stood behind E's shoulder and pointed at Pastor Wallace. "You fake-ass preacher! We got you! God's gonna kill you!"

"Get out of here, Roxy! Go calm down," E said. She gave the disgraced pastor a final look of disgust before turning to leave the room. Their eyes met, and she could see how scared he was, not knowing what would happen next.

"It's not what I think, huh?" E inched closer, bringing the gun to just inches from the man's face. "So, trying to stick your dick in Angela's lil sister is normal? She is a minor… and you know this!"

Realizing just how much E had the upper hand, the pastor spoke slowly and began to apologize. "You're absolutely right. No need to deny it. I'm sorry I took it a little too far."

"Sit your ass in that chair over there." E pointed the gun and watched the older man stand and walk to a straight wood chair. "I'm shocked at you," he said with disdain. "I looked up to you as a respectable elder."

"I can understand that, E," the pastor said carefully, his hands still raised.

"Shut your damn mouth! Big fucking sins been committed, pastor man! Sexual assault, attempted rape on a minor." E saw the pastor's expression grow more and more troubled as he counted down the list of possible charges. "Your ass need to be taxed. You a phony!"

"Son, my people... my congregation can't ever find out about what took place... *especially* Isaiah," Pastor Wallace pleaded.

"I'm no son to a rapist!" E said. "And you better stay out the presence of my Pop, 'cause I can't see him dealing with a fucking pedophile."

"No problem, son," the pastor said. "Can we settle this like businessmen?" He paused a moment to study E's face and then continued, "I can give you five hundred thousand on Monday, in the Publix lot on Piedmont. That should take care of the damages in a big way. Again... I am *so* sorry."

"Shit! Nah pastor, you talking a little light. You want this to go away, a million is the payoff. Half a mil on Monday, and then fifty thousand every month for the next ten months." E laughed, watching the color drain from Pastor Wallace's face.

"I got no problem coming up with the first half," he said, holding his hands out in a pleading gesture. "But… but the other half… would have to come from the church," he stuttered. "And that's used to assist families in need."

While he spoke, E pulled out his phone and called Angela's number. "Yo, bring me that, baby," he said and hung up. He pointed and yelled at Pastor Wallace, "Stop the bullshit, man! This ain't no debate. You got no damn *assistance program*. You and your proud-to-the-core wife gives less than a *fuck* about your people!"

"What? No, I…"

"See, pastor man, you like popping little girls. It's time for animals like you to be put on a tight leash before you die. A lil grace period is all it is." E stood again and pointed the gun directly at him, watching him sweat and heave deep breaths. "Repent, muthafucker!"

From where he sat, Pastor Wallace could see Angela walk into the room from behind E. Her face was twisted in a hateful expression, and she glared at him with fire in her eyes. In her hand was a gold disc. "Play that shit for him, baby," E said as Angela walked between them to place the disc into the dvd player on the television.

"My pleasure. Catching a traitor like you is something special," she said to the pastor.

"Excuse me? You're calling me a traitor?" he asked.

"Damn right! Taking people's money so you and your raggedy snow bunny can live a lavish life. That shit is over with."

The room was silent for a few seconds, but then the events from the past hour began to replay on the tv screen. "You see that shit?" E looked at the pastor while pointing to the television. "You bit off too much fucking cake, pervert!" Defeated, Pastor Wallace lowered his head in shame.

"Remember, ten o'clock Monday morning. And don't come up short." E walked to the front door and opened it wide. "Now get out."

*****

The standing-room-only crowd grew quiet when J took center stage. The room was dimly lit, but he could see only attentive faces as he began.

Sex is good – it has its place

Some men and women play it like a sport Unconscious minds sexing one another back and forth

Sexual gain above anything

Late night, unprotected fuck sessions…

E was alone in his car, driving along a dark road in another part of town. Traffic was light, so he punched the gas.

Hardcore, deep throat – what you thought! Looking for thrills

Threesomes on the regular, perfecting their skills

Nymphos and fornicators be getting' it in, habitual sex addicts

Habits they won't break, freakish ways

No commitments, just one volunteer who don't care

Chlamydia kings and queens

STDs worn with pride the new trend in 2010

The hell with what God say. I fear not

Lust over loyalty is what some men live by

A woman's flesh, ass and breast

Body well-equipped Nymphos knows this…

Angela relaxed and leaned back in the warm bathwater. She reached over the bubbles to grab a glass of wine from the side of the tub. Roxy was out of the house visiting friends, and E had gone to handle some business.

He better come strong, penis long, doggie style spread them

cheeks,

    'Cause she like to be penetrated deep

    With roughness

    Strong backs enjoy dishing out pain

    No question when it comes to sluts

    It brings on massive nuts

    White cream nympho favorite

    Lick it around her lips Dietary supplement…

E saw the entrance sign to a neighborhood up ahead and slowed down. He turned into a subdivision and a few houses in, he turned off the street and rolled slowly into a driveway. He got out of the car and began walking toward the house, but it opened before he could reach the front door. Honey, the female from a few nights back at The Spot, was standing in the doorway. She was wearing a seductive smile and not much else. E smiled back and tugged at the hem of her lingerie as he walked inside.

    Dogs in heat is all they would ever be

    Her punisher. The man that brings the thunder

    Her magic stick. Number on. Her top ten list

Honey closed the door behind them, then grabbed E by the arm and pulled him toward a back room. "Hey. I been waiting for you all day."

"I'm here now." E looked at the curves of her body. "Damn, you look good!"

*****

"Shit! Look at that," Carlos said, sucking his teeth. "Nine forty-five a.m., and they standing out there like they got a crack dealer license." He and Isaiah were sitting in a vehicle outside of a known dope house. He looked at a picture of their suspect. "Ervin Samuels, a-k-a Black. Nowhere to be found," he said impatiently.

"Well, this is the only tip we got… Mr. Black's money spot," Isaiah responded.

Carlos eyed the males standing along the street and on the corner near the house. "What the hell is wrong with these kids?" He nodded toward one in particular. "Tattoos on his face like he lost his mind. He ugly now, so just wait 'til he get to be our age!" he said, shaking his head.

"They look at life from a different perspective than we do," Isaiah said.

"Ha! You're right. Thinking it's okay to fuck up your face is a whole different perspective! He missing some marbles."

Isaiah looked on with a frown. "Yeah, racking up gun charges and being a clown is easy to do in America."

Chapter Twelve

Pastor Wallace pulled up to the meeting spot and saw E's car there, already parked. He stopped next to the passenger side where E was sitting and waited for him to let down his window. As soon as it came down, he handed E a brown paper bag.

"We looking good?" E took the bag without looking inside. He stared directly in Pastor Wallace's eyes.

"It's all there." The pastor watched E pass the bag to the guy sitting behind the wheel of his car.

"Look," E said and leaned back to give the pastor a clear view of the other person in the car. "I need for you to meet somebody."

"Que pasa," the guy said with a deadly stare.

"Next month, same time and place. Make sure he get that," E said, nodding toward the driver but never taking his eyes off the pastor. "Feel me?"

"Yeah, I feel you. One down and ten more to go." Without another word, Wallace shifted his car into gear and drove away.

*****

Ervin Samuels, a-k-a Black, stood in the middle of a clothing store watching the two females that were with him as they tore through the racks of clothes. Each one had a pile of items folded over one arm. The phone vibrated in his front pocket. "Hello."

"Them folks at you dog," said a gravelly voice. "Bounty hunters came round earlier looking for you."

"For sure?" Black turned in a circle, looking around at the other people in the store.

"No bullshit. They got the spot hot," the caller said with an icy tone. "This is shit we don't need. I made myself clear way back. You better handle your problem. Feel me?" Before Black could answer, the line went dead.

Back in front of the dope spot, Carlos and Isaiah suddenly felt uneasy. The thugs in front of the house began to stir and look and point at them. "You can have a wonderful plan, but when it don't turn out the way you thought, it makes you study the picture a little harder," Isaiah said. He looked from side to side and to the back of the vehicle to try and keep an eye on everybody around the car.

"Like you tell all of us… the Father has it all in control." Carlos looked at the guys around them with a laugh. "Look at these clowns. Smoke some blunts, pop some pills… but now they got heart."

"Wait." Isaiah held up his hand to get Carlos' attention. A young couple walked directly toward them, prompting them to open the doors and get out of the car.

"Is there a problem?" Carlos asked with a hand on his gun.

"We told you that nigga ain't here," the guy spoke up in a hostile tone.

Isaiah stared him down. "So, you coming back with temper tantrums, young man?"

"You and fucking Poncharello need to get out the hood before something knock you down!"

"You better think twice before you try us," Isaiah said. "I'll have DEA on this block before your little witch can roll your next blunt," he said, pointing to the young girl.

"What are you saying?! I'll swing on your ass! Think I won't, old man?" The girl suddenly stepped forward and made a bucking motion toward Isaiah.

Carlos gripped the handle of his gun even tighter. Seeing this, the guy held an arm out in front of his companion. "Cool it, sis!"

"Threats from a small fry? Listen to your ace boon coon.

You don't wanna do that," Carlos told the girl.

"Come on." The guy stood in front of the girl and started pushing her backward, back down the street. "Let's go! Shut yo ass up!" he shouted when she hesitated to move her feet.

"Remember this number…" Carlos shouted behind them, "… 6-7-8, 4-3-2, 1-2-1-2. Call me when Black shows up!"

"And if I have to come back tomorrow, I'll be right here with the DEA unit locking all y'alls asses up!" Isaiah shouted before getting back into the vehicle and slamming the door.

*****

Rebbie reached up into the closet in E's old room to pull down some of his old clothes and shoes. She had spent most of the afternoon packing up his things, and finally made her way to the back of the closet. She found an old shoebox and opened it to see old pictures of the boys – baby and school portraits, and even some old hunting photos. Smiling, she sat on the bed so she could empty the box and spread them out. "Them boys are not little no more," she sighed. "My big boys." She came across a sheet of paper that was folded in half. It was the old letter of agreement between E and J from five years earlier, for ownership of the family business. Rebbie unfolded the paper and read out loud. "I, E Jones, on the 23rd day of February 2005, give inheritance - *slash* - full ownership to J Jones." The words of the agreement sank in, and she sat there staring at the page with tears welling up in her eyes.

*****

Angela and Roxy stood behind E, watching him count money at the dining table. After a while, he turned to Roxy and put a stack of cash in her hand. "There's five thousand dollars," he said. "Go buy whatever you want."

"Ooh, that's what I'm saying!" Her eyes got big. "It's time to go shopping! Thanks, big bro!"

"Mmm-hmm..." Angela looked at Roxy and rolled her eyes. "Don't start smelling your lil ass 'cause you got some money."

"Please, Angela! What you take me for? Cool out with that shit," Roxy responded by rolling her eyes and waving a hand in her big sister's direction.

"Listen to your sister, Roxy. Don't spend this money like you stupid, 'cause I got no problem cutting you off," E said.

"I won't. My job is done. That pervert caught a big loss fucking with us." Roxy turned to leave. "I gotta go get ready.

146

Cynthia 'bout to pick me up." She stopped to hug E and Angela on her way out of the room.

"Hey! Answer your phone when I call… and have your ass back here tonight! No sleepovers!" Angela called after her little sister. When Roxy didn't answer, she shook her head and looked back to where E was still counting money.

"I got some business to handle tonight, so don't wait up," he said without looking up from the table.

"So where were you Saturday and Sunday night?

Fucking two or three bitches?"

"What you say?" E turned to look at her.

"Don't be fucking no other pussy when I'm not there, E! When you start slinging, I gotta be there!" She tried hard to keep the emotion out of her voice.

"Who need *you* to fuck some pussy?" he asked sarcastically. "I do the damn sticking. God gave me a nightstick that puts you to sleep every time. How the fuck you sound? I know what to do with tits and ass."

Angela walked right up to him, staring at his neck. "Look! That bitch bit your ass up! You got red marks on your neck. You let a ho bite you like that?!"

"You see it! And… *what*?" E stood up from the table. "I'm in charge of things. And the same thing applies to you *and* Roxy. I'll cut you off." He stared Angela down to make sure his point was made.

"Fuck you, E!" she yelled and turned to walk away. E grabbed her arm and tried to pull her close, but she jerked away.

"You heard what I said. I got no time for hard-headed chicks!"

Angela smirked. "Say it! You wanna call me a bitch. That's what you wanna say!" she screamed. She left the room in a rage, waving her arms and cursing in Spanish.

"Say that shit in English, not Spanish!"

*****

Isaiah gazed at his wife across the dinner table. The lights were low, and candlelight flickered between them while classic jazz played softly throughout the restaurant. Rebbie was in the middle of telling him a story and had a smile on her face. She didn't notice how her bright smile was making him smile. "Yeah, that girl Leah is a mess!" she said, patting the table with one hand. "She said Ace asked her to bake him a cake, but she forgot. So, at the last minute, she bought one from the store. Fixed it up and then told Ace she tried a new recipe. So when he ate a piece, he said this was the best cake she ever made!"

"What?" Isaiah said, and they both laughed.

"He said *I like this! This is the best one right here!*" Isaiah shook his head. "Just hurt her feelings."

"Yeah, hurt her poor lil feelings. But she couldn't be mad at him. She thought she could trick him. But he told her to keep using the new recipe!"

Isaiah laughed, "Ace wants that cake out of the store and don't even know it!"

"Leah had me crying, baby. I told her don't be like a lot of black women get mad and run that man away. Society tricked a whole lot of sister's out of a black man."

"Hillary still have Bill." She knows not to leave." "Mmm-hmm, that's for sure," Isaiah laughed. Then her tone turned more serious. "But your Pastor Wallace, he got a bigger one. The First Lady been calling me ever since Friday." Isaiah frowned and asked, "Who and what slipped up?"

"Well, seem like she caught him talking in code to some female on the phone. But when she asked him about it, he said it was Brother Matthew."

Isaiah shrugged. "Well… maybe so."

"First Lady ain't falling for that one. She told me, Thursday night he goes out and put on cologne he don't even wear for her. Come back the next morning looking all crazy in the face, telling her it's time to cut back on shopping." Rebbie leaned forward, "Guess why."

"Why?"

"He said the Lord told him she need to cut back." They looked at each other and laughed again.

"She does wear a lot of makeup," Isaiah said, lifting his eyebrows.

"Yes, Lord!" Rebbie agreed. "And that war paint is

expensive!" Then her look turned serious again. "She asked me if I thought he was committing adultery."

"Oh yeah? What did you tell her?"

"I told her that's her man, so *she* should know."

Isaiah smiled and laid down his napkin. "You don't believe in sugar-coating nothing, huh baby?"

"She know him better than me! My only concern is you and me."

"Oh boy! If he is sneaking around with women, that's a big violation."

Isaiah realized one of their favorite songs was playing, Barry White's "I'll Always Love You." He reached across the table and took Rebbie's hand.

"I'm just happy to see you smile," Rebbie said. "The last few days, you haven't been yourself. I'm used to having my daddy give me a smile every day."

Isaiah gave her a sly grin. "What else do you want Daddy to give you?"

"I want you to take me home and hold me in your arms before Rachel the Opera Singer warms up."

*****

J was in the car outside of his parent's house, waiting for Rachel to come out. Inside, Rachel walked around gathering her things

for the day. It was early, so she sang softly to herself, thinking

150

she wouldn't disturb anyone. *"Oh yeah, do me, baby"* she sang, walking into the kitchen. Rebbie walked into the room at the same time. "Good morning," Rebbie said.

"Oh! Good morning, Mom."

"I see you *love* singing. You sing morning, noon and night, don't you?"

"You can tell?" Rachel asked, smiling sweetly. "Oh yeah. I hear you all the time."

Rebbie looked around and asked, "Where's J?"

"In the car waiting. I'm taking him to work 'cause I got a ten o'clock appointment to look at a house."

"Oh yeah?"

"Yes, ma'am. A two-bedroom townhome." "That's good, baby," Rebbie said with a smile.

"Well, let me get out of this car before he start blowing."

"Yeah, you right," Rebbie said laughing. "Have a nice day, baby."

"You too, Mom. Love you!"

"Love you, too!" Rebbie watched Rachel walk toward the door. "And cut down on the singing, baby."

Outside, J leaned over and opened the door for Rachel. She jumped in and tossed her purse and other belongings into the back seat. Hearing a favorite song on the radio, she turned up the volume and started to bob her head. "Mom said she hear me singing all the time," she said with a smile.

J broke out laughing and touched her arm. "Mom ain't talking about *that* kind of singing."

"What?!" Rachel shrieked. "Mom be hearing us? Oh my goodness! I'm so embarrassed!" She covered her mouth with her hands. "Wait… and I asked her could she tell I like to sing!" She fell back against her seat and swatted a hand at J. "Stop laughing! It's not funny!"

"Calm down, baby," he said, still laughing. "But I definitely gotta get our own spot now."

Rachel sat with her arms folded across her chest. "Your mom played me. She something else!"

"Yeah baby, you got played."

*****

J sat at a desk alone in the bonding office. His thought had been to come in early before everyone else to handle some paperwork before things got busy. But instead, he had spent the last hour spinning around in the desk chair with the memories of recent events turning over and over in his mind. Suddenly the phone rang and broke his train of thought. "Jones Bail Bonds, how may I help you?"

"Hey handsome," a seductive female voice said, "y'all still looking for that scumbag, Black?"

"Damn, sweetheart! That's how you feel about him?" "Sure do!" she said with a laugh. "3-2-7 Glenwood Avenue in Decatur is where you can find that asshole!"

152

Before J could ask a question or say anything else, the line clicked and went dead. "Black, you crossed the *wrong,* sista," he said, writing the address on a notepad. "3-2-7 Glenwood Ave. Let me hit Pops up." He reached for his phone and called Isaiah.

"Yeah J, what you got?" Isaiah answered the phone that was mounted to the dashboard of his vehicle. He and Carlos were in the car and could hear J clearly through the speaker.

"I just spoke to a angry Black woman with a new address on Black. Decatur, 3-2-7 Glenwood Avenue."

Isaiah hit the steering wheel with his fist. "Yes! That's what I been waiting for!" He and Carlos exchanged looks and nodded. "So, one of Mr. Samuels' women dropped a dime on him," he said with a grin. "Okay, son. We're headed over there right now." He hung up the call and looked back at Carlos. "Hopefully, we got a break."

"Your bullshit is starting to smell, Mr. Black," Carlos said. He braced himself with a hand against the dashboard as Isaiah whipped the car around to go in the opposite direction.

Chapter Thirteen

Black let the warm water inside the shower hit his face and run down his chest while the woman in front of him slowly massaged and kissed the front of his body. He leaned his head back and reached to grab the soft female body that was behind him. Both women giggled and moaned each time their own hands touched as they caressed Black between them. He smiled, completely relaxed and enjoying their three-way session when he heard what sounded like a knock on the front door. He held up one hand, motioning for the women to be quiet. And there it was again. Definitely a knock, and much harder the second time.

"Man, I bet that's them folks! Marvin snitched!" he said, stepping out of the shower. Looking back, he told one of the females, "Tina, you stay in here with the water running. Nicole," he said to the other one, "you go answer the door and stall them muthafuckers while I hide in the closet. You know what to tell 'em." Nicole grabbed a towel and wrapped it around her body before heading to the front door. Black grabbed a towel along with a gun and ran into a bedroom closet.

Another hard knock sounded throughout the house as Nicole approached the door. She looked through the peephole to see two Black men wearing holsters standing on the porch. One seemed to be staring right back at her through the peephole. "Who is it?" she called out.

"Bounty agents! Open the door, please!"

She undid the locks and opened the door slightly, just enough to show that she wasn't dressed. "Yes, can I help you?"

"Isaiah Jones, bounty agent. We have a warrant for Black. We got information that he's here."

"Well, that's the wrong damn information. He don't live here," Nicole said with an ice-cold stare.

"Do you know him?" Isaiah asked.

"No, I don't," she said. "So go bang on somebody else's door."

"You sure about that?" Isaiah asked, raising an eyebrow.

"Because if you're lying to me, it won't be good for you." "I don't like repeating myself."

Isaiah looked at his shoes and shook his head. "Okay, so you're sticking with that, huh? I'm gonna take a look anyway." He drew his pistol and then used one hand to push the door open. He and Carlos stepped past Nicole and into the house.

She stomped her foot and yelled, "I got rights! Y'all can't just bust up in here! I told your crooked ass I don't know no Black!" She grabbed the front of her towel and motioned toward the back of the house. "Me and my baby was in the shower, and here y'all come with this bullshit!"

"It won't take long," Carlos assured her. He crossed the room to check behind a sofa and set of long drapes.

"Damn! Can't you just take my word?"

The two men looked at each other and laughed, and Isaiah came and stood in front of her. "Miss, what's your name again?"

"I never told you."

"I'm sorry. I thought you did," he said.

"No, I didn't. But if you need to know, it's Paula." "Okay, Paula. I promise it won't take but a minute."

Isaiah turned to his partner. "Carlos, check the rooms in the back."

"Bet," Carlos said with a nod.

Isaiah gave Nicole a steady and stern look. "We got a tip that he stays here. We know Ervin Samuels is his real name."

"Ha! Whoever gave you that tip lied."

"Uh-huh…" Isaiah looked her up and down and noticed that she wouldn't maintain eye contact. He knew instinctively by the way her eyes darted from side to side that she was hiding something, or someone. Carlos made his way toward the back of the house, checking under beds and inside closets from room to room as he moved down the hallway. Black watched from inside a closet as Carlos entered one of the bedrooms. Carlos kneeled to look under the bed, and then stood to walk in Black's direction. Inches from grabbing the closet door, Carlos turned abruptly when a female voice caught his ear from another room. Black let out a long, deep breath and released the grip on his gun as Carlos left the bedroom to find the source of the voice he'd heard.

"Baby, what's going on?" Tina yelled from inside the shower. Hearing footsteps enter the bathroom, she pulled back the curtain.

"Oh! I'm sorry, ma'am!" Carlos stepped back in shock.

"What the fuck?! Who are you?" Tina grabbed the edge of the curtain and tried to cover her naked body.

"Bounty agent, ma'am. I got a warrant for Ervin Samuels."

"He damn sure ain't in here! Get the hell out! You got the wrong house!"

Back in the front room, Isaiah noticed a pair of men's athletic shoes by a chair. He looked back at the woman in front of him and said coolly, "I guess you were right. Sorry for the inconvenience."

"Told you! Now can you please leave, 'cause my shower's getting cold."

Isaiah looked past her and yelled to his partner, "Carlos, everything clear?"

"All clear," Carlos said, walking back into the room.

Isaiah noticed a strange look on his face.

"I appreciate it, ma'am. Here's my card," Isaiah said to Nicole.

"Yes, ma'am. We apologize," Carlos said as he walked out onto the front porch.

"Get the hell out! Told you, ain't no fugitives in here."

The two men walked back to their car in silence. Once inside the vehicle, Isaiah turned and asked, "You sure you checked those rooms good?"

"They were clear. Checked the bathroom, too. Ran up on something, but it wasn't no man. I was like *Whoa*!" Carlos said, holding both hands up in front of him.

"She has a *woman* as her man?" Isaiah asked.

"That's what came out from behind the shower curtain. *Nice* breasts, bro!" Carlos turned his hands like he was cupping a pair of breasts.

"Nah… you can believe that garbage if you want to, but I'm telling you, he's in there. I saw a pair of men's gym shoes in the front room. So all we have to do is wait a few hours. He'll show his face."

"Mister Black got his women playing games for him," Carlos said, staring at the house.

"Everybody like to act. It's their job."

*****

The lights were dim in Honey's living room, and a mix of R&B and hip-hop was coming from the speakers. He reclined on the couch with Honey and stroked her body as she laid wet kisses on his lips and neck. Then, the sound of his phone buzzing on the coffee table broke the mood. E grabbed it and, seeing it was Ben, answered and put it on speaker. "Yeah."

"We got a problem," Ben said. "Talk to me."

"Sareed got hit up early this morning."

E pushed Honey to the side and sat up. "Where? At the store?" "At his crib."

"Where you at?" E glanced at his phone to check the time.

"Me and Antonio on our way to Gwinnett."

"I'll be there." E hung up the call. "*Damn*," he said under his breath.

Honey smiled and reached to massage his shoulders. "On the move again, huh?"

"I gotta do it while I'm young, so when I'm older everything will be in order."

"I hope I'm included…" she let the words trail off like a question.

E looked her in the eye and said with a smirk, "You can be my jump off. I jump on you whenever I wanna release some stress." He stood up from the couch and straightened his clothes. Honey sat and stared up at him.

"Ride me like a horse," she said. "I got enough room on this big ass, and it's all yours."

*****

Kenya came to a stretch in the road where no cars were coming and dialed the office from the phone on her dashboard. There were two rings before J picked up on the other end. "What's up, nephew? You busy up in there?" she asked.

"How you doing, Auntie? I ain't trying to hear that," J laughed. "When you getting back in here?"

"It's like that? Y'all miss me?" Kenya asked sarcastically.

"Shoot… miss you helping me with the phones and paperwork."

"Tell Jo-Jo I said hey," she said with a laugh. "Kenya said *hey*, Uncle Jo-Jo."

"What's good, lil sis?" Kenya could hear Jo-Jo's voice getting

159

louder as he walked toward the phone. "How 'bout picking me up ten two-dollar jumbo scratch-offs?"

"I know you heard that," J said to her. "Yeah, loud and clear." She rolled her eyes and smiled at the same time. "Tell him I want my 20 dollars when I see him, 'cause he ain't won nothing over the last few months." She heard J repeating her words to Joe, "Kenya said you gotta pay up when she see you."

"*Shit*! That's all you want is twenty dollars out of fifty g's when I hit? More for me!"

"Tell Jo-Jo be quiet! I want half! Shoot, I'm putting up the money. He hit, I hit. Don't even play!"

*****

Out of the closet, Black sat on the side of the bed and dialed a number on his phone. After several rings, there was a female voice on the other end. "Hello!"

"It's like that, huh? That's how you get down?" "Who is this?"

Black looked at his phone, dumbfounded. He had just been with this female at the drug spot. "Y'all snitching niggas got it coming, yo."

"What the hell are you talking about? You got the wrong number, man."

"Bitch, where the hell is Marvin?!" Black yelled into the phone.

"I got your bitch!" she shouted back. "Listen, nigga… don't no Marvin stay here! And never dial this number again. *And* you better leave them drugs alone!" She hung up and turned to a guy that was standing by listening. "See how I played stupid with Black? *You dialed the wrong number, nigga!*" They both laughed and pounded fists.

"Nigga better get ready for prison and leave them fine ass hos for me to fuck," the guy said, taking a long drag from the cigarette in his hand.

Furious, Black sat for a few seconds and then walked into the dining room. He took a seat at the table where Nicole and Tina were already sitting in silence. "We need to bounce out this crib," he said matter-of-factly.

"How baby, with them bounty hunters outside?" Nicole asked.

"I can't let that shit stop me," he said. "Once the sun goes down, Tina can bring the car closer to the crib."

"Hell yeah! Back that shit up so we can get the hell on!" Tina bounced in her seat with excitement.

"Just make sure that back seat is clear for my boo," Nicole said, staring lovingly at Black.

"You think I won't?" Tina shot back. "Black know I got his back! Don't you, Blacky?"

"Excuse me?" Nicole said, rolling her eyes. "What was that for, bitch?"

"Kill that noise!" Black interrupted. "I'm the one with the money in this bitch, that's laying pipe to both of y'all. So, *I* ask the questions. You two just take orders." He looked back and forth between the two women who were giving each other death stares. "Tina, call and order that pizza special for seven ninety-nine. And then get whatever you want, baby. Tell them clowns to come to the side door." Nicole's stare was replaced with a stunned look as she watched a sarcastic grin spread across Tina's face.

"Sure will, Blacky. Anything for you," Tina gloated.

*****

"This better be the store, 'cause I'm tired of seeing you waste twenty bucks a day on this Lotto crap," Kenya said to Joe over the phone. "It's turning into a bad habit, Jo-Jo." She pulled her car into the parking lot of a convenience store. Unbeknownst to her, E was inside the same store in a back room with Ben, Sareed and Antonio in a tense, heated discussion.

E stared at Sareed and asked, "So we talking eighty thousand?"

"Yeah, that's right. Exactly what I give you every month. Eighty thousand dollars."

"That's all they took?" Ben asked.

"No…" Sareed was agitated and began to move his hands about wildly as he spoke. "They took my wife's sense of security! She doesn't feel safe in our house anymore. Not safe for her," he said.

"Answer the question. He ain't concerned with your *wife*," E said, sucking his teeth.

Sareed threw his hands up again. "That's all they ask for," he said. "*Give money! We know you got money. You make plenty*

162

money at your store! We kill your wife if you don't!"

"Were they Black, white, or Spanish?" Antonio asked. "No Spanish or white… they were Black," Sareed answered.

"How many?"

Sareed looked at Antonio and said, "Two Black guys – one tall and the other short. Short guy call out a name."

"What name did he say?" E asked. "He say *Rack!*"

E frowned. "*Rack?*"

"Yeah," Sareed nodded. "*Rack…* no, not *Rack… Rock!* That's it! *Rock.*"

E pounded the tabletop with both fists. "Bullshit! Your dogs ain't on no damn leash. You like testing a muthafucker? I'm all about that action, man!"

Out front, Kenya had been moving slowly across the front of the drink cooler. "Lemon iced tea… mango iced tea… $1.29 for some Snapple. Yep, that's what I'm saying!" She reached in and grabbed a bottle. "Now, I need some Grandma cookies and I'm straight."

Sareed shrugged with a puzzled look. "I'm sure that's what he said. You know him?"

"Don't ask me no questions," E said.

"But… I pay you for protection," Sareed said, sounding bewildered.

"Not against home invasions. That's your fucking problem."

"So… what? Just let them rob me again? Remember, it's your

money."

"You sound weak as hell," E said. "You foreigners come here, make plenty money and expect not to get touched.

Everybody gets robbed."

Not knowing what to do or say, Sareed just looked at the men around the table. E stared at him for a few seconds, and then stood. "Let's go," he said to the other two. Ben opened the door and they started to walk out into the main area of the store. Before stepping out, E heard Sareed's voice behind him.

"E…" Sareed said nervously, "I'm going to need a little more time on the next payment."

"What?!" E turned and made two swift steps back to where Sareed still sat at the table. "He smack you with the gun too hard?" He pointed two fingers directly at the center of Sareed's forehead. "Listen… you still got that payment to make. Same date, same amount. Have it all next time I come to collect."

Before heading to the front of the store, Kenya heard loud voices coming from the back and turned to see E and several other young guys standing around a doorway. She hid behind a food shelf and stayed out of sight to try and hear what was going on - yelling about a robbery and some kind of payment. "What the hell is E into, extortion?" she whispered aloud.

Ben poked Sareed's chest with his finger. "Fuckin bumbaclot! Don't fuck wit' us!" He followed E and the rest of the crew out of the store.

*****

Isaiah and Carlos sat parked near Black's residence and watched a pizza delivery vehicle drive past them and then slowly come to a stop in front of the house. "You see Carlos, this younger generation eat garbage all day every day. The women don't cook, and that's fine with the men."

"Damn! Predictable dummies," Carlos said, shaking his head.

Inside the house, Black heard a loud knock. He grabbed his gun and moved toward the door. "Who is it?!"

"Pizza delivery!"

Black opened the door. "How much?"

The young guy looked at the receipt taped to the top of the box. "Uh… Nineteen sixty-eight, sir."

Black reached into his front pocket and pulled out two bills. He handed them over and grabbed the box. "Here's thirty. Keep the change."

"Appreciate that!" The kid's eyes lit up and he nodded his head. "Dude knows how to tip!" He stuffed the money into his pocket and then hopped off the side of the porch and jogged back to his car.

"When he comes back this way, flag him down," Isaiah said. Carlos got out of the car and waved to the delivery guy just as he was driving past. He came to an abrupt stop, and Carlos approached the car and showed his badge.

"Bounty agent," he said as the boy let down his window. He

165

held up a picture of Black. "Did you see this guy at the house you just came from?"

The kid squinted at the photo and said, "Yeah, he paid for a large pizza."

"Are you sure it was this guy?"

"Hell yeah, dude! He gave me a ten-dollar tip!" "Alright. Thanks for your cooperation." Carlos took a step back and hit the top of the car. He walked back to the SUV and got inside. "He's in there," he said, nodding towards the house. "You were right. The dumb ass paid for it."

Isaiah chuckled. "Let him eat that first slice. Then we knock."

Inside the house, Tina and Nicole sat on the couch with Black eating pizza and watching tv. Nicole kept looking back and forth from the television to Black's face. "Black, don't you think we should be getting the hell outta here?"

"Shut up and eat, 'fore I shove this slice down your throat" was his only answer.

"Would you please?! That mouth!" Tina chimed in.

Suddenly, there was another hard knock on the door. When they heard "Bounty agent! Open up!" they froze and looked at each other.

"Dammit!" Nicole said. "I *knew* we should'a *been* gone… sitting here eating some damn pizza!"

Black got up and started toward the kitchen. "I'm going out the back door," he said in a calm, even tone. "Tina, pick me up around the corner. Nicole, make them muthafuckers wait… stall 'em as long as you can."

Carlos stood right outside the front door with Isaiah in the yard close to the porch. He banged on the door a second time. "Bounty agent! Open up! Open the door!" They both heard a door slam from the back of the house.

"He ran out the back door! I'll get him, you check the house," Isaiah yelled and ran toward the back yard in time to see Black running into some bushes.

Bam-Bam-Bam-Bam! Carlos pounded on the front door again. "Open the damn door, or I will kick it open!" He stepped back ready to strike the door with his boot when suddenly it opened, and a young woman stood there with an annoyed expression. He immediately recognized her as the same female who opened the door the last time they came to the house. "Back up! Back up! Where is he?" he shouted, pushing past her into the house.

"Who, muthafucker?!"

Once inside, Carlos saw Tina swipe keys from a kitchen counter and run out of the back door. He caught sight of Isaiah chasing Black as he ran through yards and hopped fences trying to escape. "You fucked up, Paula!" he yelled to the girl now standing behind him in the kitchen. "You're under arrest."

"For what?!"

"Don't play with me. Black was here. Aiding and abetting a fugitive," he said while putting handcuffs on her. "Where's your partner?”

“Don’t ask me shit!”

*****

“Where you at, Black? Come on Baby, show yourself” Tina mumbled as she drove slowly through the neighborhood. She had no way of knowing that Black was only a few hundred feet away from her, crouched against the back of an empty house. Isaiah was still chasing him with a flashlight and was closing in.

The beam from the flashlight was hitting objects all around him in the dark.

Black pulled the gun from his waistband. “That nigga gotta go.”

“Black, give yourself up! All this running and hiding ain’t worth it!” Isaiah yelled. Black could hear Isaiah’s footsteps in the gravel along the side of the house and knew he was less than five feet away.

“Fuck you, nigga!” Black stepped out from behind the wall and fired two shots. *Bang-Bang*! He ran off into the darkness without seeing Isaiah stumble backwards and fall, hitting his head on a large stone in the yard. Isaiah managed to shoot off one round before he hit the ground. A couple of blocks away, Carlos was putting Nicole into the truck, and they both heard the gunfire.

“You heard that shit?” she sneered. “Your partner is dead. That’s what y’all niggas get!”

“You better hope not, for your sake.” Carlos shoved her inside

168

and slammed the door. He jumped into the vehicle, sped to the end of the block, and then turned in the direction of the gunshots. After driving a short distance, he slowed down and started looking from one side of the street to the other. He rolled up to a man standing on the curb in front of what looked like an abandoned house. The man was wearing dark clothes that helped his black skin almost blend into the night. As Carlos was driving by, he started waving his arms.

"Hey man," he said. "That's your partner back there? I think he got shot."

Carlos slammed on brakes. "Where?"

"On the side of the house back there," he said, pointing toward the backyard. "That's where the shots came from."

"I told you, muthafucker! We some killers! I hope he's dead!" Nicole yelled from the back seat.

Carlos reached around and slapped her face. "Enough with the tough talk!"

"Aw shit, you fucking spick!" she shouted.

Carlos got out and secured the vehicle before pulling his gun and running to the side of the house. There was no light between the yards, but a few yards ahead, he saw what looked like a body on the ground. "Isaiah! Oh shit!" He yelled and ran to his side.

Carlos knelt beside Isaiah and could see, feel, and smell a lot of blood. "Damn! Hang in there… It's not your time yet! Not yet!"

A couple of blocks away, Tina had heard the shots, too. She

was rounding another corner when her phone rang. It was Black. "Where you at?" he asked in a hoarse whisper.

"Crossing over Morgan Place."

"Turn around and come back to Hooper. I'll be waiting up the block.

*****

E, Antonio, and Ben walked up to an apartment and Antonio knocked on the door. They could hear loud rap music from inside. "Who is it?" a female voice yelled from the other side of the door.

"It's Earl! Rock here?" Antonio answered. "He ain't here. What you need?"

"Some loud."

"Hold on," she said. As soon as the door opened slightly, the three of them rushed forward and forced their way into the apartment. The woman screamed and stood trembling with both hands in the air.

"Yo! Get the fuck down!" Ben yelled. "Who else in here?"

She slowly got down on both knees while looking at each of their faces. Her eyes got big when they rested on E's face. "E… what the fuck you doing?"

"Where's Rock, Coco… and my money?"

Her expression suddenly turned from one of fear to bravado. "He ain't here, white boy! I'm here by myself." She looked at the other two again. "Rock is gonna *murder* you."

"Get her up and take her to the bedroom," E said. He told Ben,

170

"Turn the music up." Antonio grabbed Coco's elbow and jerked her up from the floor. On the way to the bedroom, E stopped in the bathroom. He saw a curling iron propped against the mirror that was already plugged in. Flipping the switch to ON, he bobbed his head as the music got even louder. Walking into the bedroom, he got right in front of Coco's face. "When's the last time you saw Rock, bitch! And don't fucking lie to me!"

"I don't remember," she answered without flinching. "You talked to that bastard last night!"

"Is you deaf, cracker? *Wanna-be* nigga. I *said* I don't remember." She rolled her eyes and smirked as E backed up and paced from one side of the room to the other.

"You ask a simple question and get attitude." He shook his head and looked at Coco. "I can't be civil with you." He quickly raised his gun and took two steps to put it against her head. "Ohhh... you scared now?" he laughed, seeing her frightened expression. "I just want Rock – not you. But I will squeeze on you... then find your daughter and do the same. I want you to call that piece of shit and tell him you need some more smoke."

Coco nervously looked around the room until she spotted her phone on the bed. Breathing heavily, she grabbed it and called Rock's number. E could tell by the look on her face that it went straight to voicemail. Still pointing the gun in her direction, he motioned with his head for her to leave a message.

"Hey baby, I need some more. We all out. Niggas came

through and got all that shit. Hit me back." She hung up the call and gave E a shrug.

"Tee off on this bitch, dawg," E said to Ben and walked back to the bathroom. He heard several loud slaps and punches, and Coco screaming from the other room.

"Time to recognize, bitch," Ben said while he and Antonio kept landing blows. He punched her again, hard in the face.

"E, please... please!" Coco wailed. "I'll suck all three of y'alls dicks! I promise I don't know what Rock did. It's been three days since he's been here."

"Oh, now I get a answer?" E said, coming back into the room. "I actually ain't got time for a blowjob. Rock said you was trash anyway." Antonio and Ben both laughed.

"You still can't believe or trust a ho, dawg," Antonio said.

"Specially a proud one," E nodded.

Ben crossed his arms and eyed Coco up and down. "Baddest bitch ye say. She got that fire pussy!"

"She used to brag on her pussy, dawg. Tell dudes she got that fire," E said. "I'm 'bout to make it hotter, though. Gag that ho." He walked back to the bathroom and grabbed the curling iron that had been heating up the whole time. When he came back into the room, Coco's eyes stretched wide in terror. She struggled and tried to break free from Ben and Antonio, who were holding her arms. E used one hand to yank her shorts and panties down, and he brought the curling iron closer to the skin between her legs.

"No-no-no-no-no…" she shook her head and begged repeatedly with tears running down her face. Her cries were muffled by the rag being held over her mouth.

"Watch me make this pussy pop, dawg." Without flinching, E shoved the hot metal into Coco's vagina and smirked at the blood curdling sounds she made as she kicked and strained even more before finally falling to her knees. Ben let the rag fall to the floor, and Coco's pitiful moans filled the air. Almost paralyzed by the pain, she rolled herself up into a ball on the floor and wept.

"Somebody smother this bitch." E stepped over her and walked out of the room.

"No problem," Antonio said. He grabbed a pillow from the bed and firmly pressed it against Coco's face.

Chapter Fourteen

"Call that nigga Rock," E said to Antonio, who was sitting beside him in the front seat of the car while Ben sat silently in the back. E stared at the side of Antonio's face while he made the call, then turned to look out the window when he hung up without saying anything. "Try him again."

Antonio called Rock's number again but hung up when the call went straight to voicemail. "Still no answer from that puta!" The three of them sat in tense silence until E's phone rang.

"Sup, J?"

E sat up straight in his seat as soon as J started to speak. His voice sounded shaky and weak, and E knew something was wrong after the first couple of words. "I got bad news. Pop got shot earlier tonight."

"What?!" E leaned forward, yelling into the phone. "Is he dead?"

"Nah… but things ain't looking too good. They got him in surgery right now."

"Where's Mom?"

"We at Grady Hospital. Everybody here."

"Who the fuck did it?" E asked through clenched teeth. There was a pause on J's end, and E could hear a change in his brother's tone.

"Oh, *now* you're concerned about what's going down over here? Don't worry, E. We got it."

"You sound stupid! Pop got hit and you say what you say… *don't worry*? You know you sound fucking dumb telling me that shit," E said, rocking back and forth.

"All this arguing is a waste of energy, man." J sounded tired.

"Shit, don't bother me none. I got plenty of it tonight! I'll see you soon," E said and hung up. Without looking at Ben or Antonio, he said, "We need to go to Grady. Pop got shot tonight."

"What?!" they said at the same time.

*****

A uniformed police officer approached the group of Isaiah's loved ones in the sitting area that was down the hall from his hospital room. He had a look of disappointment on his face. "I just got back some more info on this guy," he said, speaking directly to J, Carlos, and Joe. He flipped through a small notepad and continued, "He has two female accomplices. One's name is Nicole Washington."

Carlos shook his head. "She told us her name was Paula."

"Don't she wish," the officer replied. "Nicole Washington, and the other one is Tina Dunbar."

"Yeah, I got a good look at her from head to toe," Carlos said.

"You got an address for Tina?" Joe asked.

The officer closed his pad and shook his head. "We couldn't pull anything on Tina. The address you had for Nicole is the only one we have.

J had been leaning against the wall listening. "Who he banging with? Crip...? Blood?"

"No gang ties," the officer said. "Just some wanna-be dope dealer with a gun."

Just then, Isaiah's doctor entered the room and walked toward the group, which also included Leah, Kenya, and Rachel. J stepped forward and asked, "What's the deal, doc? Is my father gonna make it?"

"He's going to pull through," Dr. Gibson said in a somber tone. "One bullet went straight through your father's thigh. The other was lodged in the upper left portion of his chest, just inches from his heart. Fortunately, we were able to remove it and stop the bleeding." He smiled at the relieved expressions of everyone standing around him. Rebbie had stepped away to pray but was now walking back into the waiting area. J reached out to pull his mother close.

"Hello, I'm Isaiah's wife," Rebbie said, nodding to the doctor.

"I'm Dr. Gibson, and I was just explaining to your son..."

"Please, no bad news," Rebbie interrupted, squeezing J's hand. Dr. Gibson gently touched her forearm.

"No, Mrs. Jones," the doctor assured her. "He's recovering, though he did lose a lot of blood. One bullet went through his upper thigh, and the other struck the upper left side of his chest, barely missing his heart. But we were able to remove it."

Rebbie clasped her hands together and rocked from side to side. "Thank you, Yahawashi! You heard my prayers!" Suddenly

Leah was beside her, and the sisters embraced each other in a tight hug.

"Amen! We thank you, Almighty Yah!" Leah said with tears in her eyes. Everyone else exchanged relieved glances and joined her in thanking the Most High.

"Carlos, did Isaiah have his vest on?" Rebbie asked.

Carlos looked down and answered with hesitation, "No. Neither one of us did. Things were moving pretty quick. He always tells me the angels have his back."

"Well, they certainly were doing their job tonight. Him being O positive, we were quickly able to replenish the blood he lost," the doctor said.

"I want to see him," Rebbie said with a hopeful expression.

"Not tonight, I'm afraid. We have to watch him closely for now. Hopefully tomorrow," the doctor replied.

Three floors below, E walked into the Emergency entrance along with Ben and Antonio. He went directly to the information desk and placed both hands on the countertop.

"Can I help you?" the female clerk asked, looking intimidated.

"My father was brought in a few hours ago from being shot. Last name Jones."

"Mr. Jones?" the clerk asked, typing into the computer. "Yeah, Isaiah Jones."

She moved the computer mouse across the desk and stared at the screen. "I see a Phillip Jones… William Jones…"

"Not him," E said, growing impatient.

"Okay… here's an older Black gentleman, but I seriously doubt he's your father, although his name *is* Isaiah Jones."

Ben slammed his fist on the counter in front of her. "Pay attention! The man did not stutter! We gon tump yah in yah face, gal!"

The young woman stared and lifted her hands in fear. "I'm so sorry! I wasn't thinking." She pointed to her left. "Go through the double doors, take the elevator to the third floor, turn right and the nurses' station will be on the left." The pale skin on her face and neck was beet red from fear and embarrassment.

"Bitch, pay attention. Don't be so quick to assume!" E gave her a cold stare before walking away.

Upstairs, Kenya grabbed Rebbie's sweater from one of the chairs in the waiting area and draped it over her shoulders as they walked to one side of the room. "Where's E?" she asked.

Rebbie shrugged. "J called him, so I'm sure he is on his way. We gotta pray as a family. That's our only hope."

"Isaiah's life was spared because it just wasn't his time. When Jo-Jo called me, I was just getting back in town from the beach," Kenya said.

"And Isaiah was missing you, in his own way. He said, '*Kenya need to hurry back 'cause these days ain't moving fast enough*'." They both laughed.

"Yeah, that sound just like him!" Then Kenya's expression

changed and she said, "I know this probably ain't the best time, but I need to talk to you."

"What is it? You sure it can wait?" Rebbie asked. "Yeah, it's nothing major. Just a lil woman talk, sis." "Okay. Well, whenever you are ready, let me know," Rebbie said.

Kenya offered a warm smile. "One thing at a time. Let's deal with what's important right now."

Suddenly E and his comrades came walking down the hallway. "Here comes my son. Oh! E, baby I'm glad you here," Rebbie said, throwing both arms around him. "Hey boys," she said, greeting Ben and Antonio. They both leaned in for a quick hug and asked how she was doing. She could only shrug and offer a weak smile.

"Hey, E. Glad you are here for your mom," Kenya said and gave him a tight hug.

"Of course!" E said before taking Rebbie's hand and leading her off to one side.

"How is he?" he asked his mother.

"Doctor says he's going to make it."

"Good," he sighed and made a praying motion with his hands. "You been in to see him?"

"No, the doctor said not tonight. But I'm staying here in case anything changes."

E felt a hand on his shoulder and turned to get a hug from his twin. "What's up, bruh?" J asked.

"What's up, lil bruh?" E looked around the room and lowered

his voice. "I don't like this shit. Come holla at me.

Excuse us, Mama." He and J stepped away and started to walk down a hallway.

"Who did it?"

"Some dope dealer who like that gunplay," J said.

E stopped walking and looked at his brother. "I asked for his name, not what he likes to do."

"If you had some real interest in Pop and the business, maybe this wouldn't have happened."

"What are you saying? *I'm* the reason he got shot?" E threw his hands up in disbelief. "*I* wasn't the one in the field with him. Who the fuck had his back?"

"He was out with Carlos," J answered. "And what, Pop wasn't wearing his vest?"

"No, not at the time."

"Where did he get shot?"

"Once in the leg, but it went straight through. And once in the shoulder- just missed his heart."

"Damn, that close?!"

"Word… that close," J said. "But all I'm saying is… money is what you seem to love more. Not the family."

E balled his fists but kept both arms at his sides. He stepped toward J. "Watch your tongue, lil bruh! You talking bout me dishonoring Pop. But do not piss me off. Don't forget I'm the oldest."

Not backing down, J took a step towards his brother. "We may be twins and true, you are the oldest. But we different, bruh. I do my best to walk on the holy side. You gravitate toward the negative - stack your cash however. I know you."

"What I seek pleasure in don't have nothing to do with Pop getting hit up." E looked J up and down with contempt. "Money is all I need – not *spoken word*. It *sound* good at the time, but that shit don't pay the bills." He looked J in the eyes and smirked, "Muthafuckers forget half the shit you say anyway."

"I spit vapors for God, not man, feel me? You know what cloth I'm cut from?"

E raised a finger to his brother's face, but then lowered his hand and shook his head. "Look man… this back and forth bullshit gonna end up leading to something. Just give up the name on this asshole so justice can be delivered for Pop. You *had* your chance."

"Nah, I'm running the show E!" J said, raising his voice. "I can't have your type of justice put the family in a bad storm."

"What?! Pop still here, so my position is solidified."

J stared at E and smiled. "Five years ago you gave that up, remember? So don't go there."

E responded by grabbing the front of J's shirt, and instantly they were grappling with E getting the upper hand. "Don't play with me, lil bruh! We ain't lil boys no more. I got no problem *removing* problems."

"Like Darius," J said matter-of-factly and felt E's anger grow even hotter. Just then, Joe rounded the corner and saw them grabbing each other.

"Hey! Hey!" Joe yelled, rushing forward. "What's wrong with y'all?! This ain't the time or the place for this shit! Isaiah would go upside both your heads! Have you two forgot how to treat each other?"

"Nah, Uncle Joe," E said. He released J's shirt and stepped back. "I'm just trying to find out who shot Pop and…" He stopped speaking when Rachel, Ben, and Antonio came into the hallway and started walking towards them. Rachel went straight to J's side and put an arm around his waist.

"You okay, baby?" she asked.

"I'm fine," he answered. Let's go back to the waiting room."

She looked into his eyes and said, "Whatever it is, don't let it get to you. Think about Pop, 'cause he needs you both. *And* your mom." She looked over her shoulder as they walked away. "E got a problem, coming up here with a attitude." E looked after them with a hard stare, but was distracted by Joe handing him a picture.

"Here… you know him? Ervin Samuels, a-k-a Black." Joe watched E's face for any trace of recognition.

"Nah, Uncle Joe. He don't look familiar," E said and looked away. He couldn't let Joe see how his spirit was stunned by seeing Black in the photo. He immediately had a flashback to the night Black shot the man at the gas station. Joe passed the picture to Ben and then to Antonio, but they both shook their heads to indicate they didn't know the man.

"Nah mon," Ben said, "but me need to meet the shotta."

*****

After checking that the coast was clear, Rock walked casually to the front door of the apartment he shared with Coco. But something was wrong – the door was standing open. He pushed it all the way open with one hand and slowly stepped inside. "Coco...! Coco! Where you at, baby?" There was no answer, but he could see light coming from the bedroom. He walked to the back room and then stood in the door speechless. Coco's body was on the floor face up, with her open eyes fixed on the ceiling. The smell of burnt flesh hung in the air, and he saw that blood stained the inside of her thighs. Rock grabbed his head and yelled, "Who the fuck burnt my girl's pussy?! Sick muthafuckers!"

****

"We can't stay here too long," Black said, grabbing Tina's thigh as they lay in bed. He raised his head to look at the clock on a nearby dresser and then let it fall back onto the pillow. "Three o'clock," he said with a deep sigh. "Them folks applying that pressure to Nicole right now, and I can't count on that bitch keeping her mouth shut."

"Relax, baby," Tina said, rolling onto her side to face him.

"Shit... I probably killed that old man last night. So you know that shit gonna' bring a lot more police, plus more charges. It's judge and jury in the street."

"Nicole ain't that stupid," Tina said. "We got our differences but when it comes to you, loyalty is top priority."

Black shook his head. "It's all about being replaced. One goes… another one step in. You made that big jump."

"It's me and you now, baby," Tina said, sliding her leg across Black's mid-section and caressing his chest. She leaned close and planted a seductive kiss on the side of his mouth.

"Roll me a blunt," he said, patting her butt. "You always rolled better than Nicole." Tina quickly sat up and then bounced from the bed to grab their stash.

"Shit… I know what to do to please my man," she said, licking her lips and smiling at him.

Chapter Fifteen

E stood beside Grandma Doli at The Spot while she counted money.

"Thomas died according to his name 'Akondo', which means ambush," she said.

"Ambush… ain't that something?" E said, shaking his head. "That's how it went down."

Grandma laid the stack of cash on the counter and continued speaking with a far-away look in her eyes. "Thomas never saw his death coming. The bastards that were sent played their role with great malice. Your father was given a second chance to live. After he recovers, things will be different. This is why the great spirit allowed him to survive - to bring change. Never question his acts but pray for answers. And forgive the man who shot your father."

"Grandma, you know how things get done these days. Been up all morning, shit just racing through my head. My Pop deserves fairness. Eye for an eye!"

Grandma Doli didn't look at E but said calmly, "Only when the creator instructs you to. I forgave Thomas' killer."

"But why?" E asked.

"I understand this is a spiritual war, these last days. And only people with a strong moral aspect will see the great spirit move amongst the evil."

"A death angel with a cause," E said.

*****

J sat at a desk in the bail bonds office, talking to his uncle Walter on the phone. "No doubt, Unc. The family been very fortunate. He's expected to recover."

"Your father is a strong man for his age, so it's up to you and E to take charge and do what's expected of you. Until Isaiah can get back on his feet."

"I'll make sure we stay on the same page," J said.

"Okay, tell your Mom to give me a call and keep me up on Isaiah's progress. I'll be praying down here."

"Okay, Unc. I'll let her know and I'll keep you on point," J said and hung up the phone.

*****

A short while later, E sat in the passenger seat while Ben drove through the city. He pulled out his phone and dialed T-Man's number.

"Hello" T-Man answered, speaking over loud hip-hop music in the background.

"T-Man, this E."

"E! What's good?"

"It's like that?" E said, sucking his teeth. "I had respect for you."

"Like what? Stop with the riddles and talk to me."

"I thought we had that mutual respect for each other," E said.

"I'm lost. I don't have a fucking clue what you saying.

My word is strong. I don't break my shit for nobody."

186

"Your flunkies… your dogs, bit me yesterday!"

T-Man sounded genuinely surprised. "Them jokers made a move on you?!"

"The wrong fucking move."

"Come talk to me. Let's say in… three hours."

"I'll be there," E said and hung up. Turning to Ben, he said, "I need to swing by the house."

*****

A nurse came and told Rebbie she could have a brief visit with her husband and led her to Isaiah's room. She entered slowly, wanting to touch him but not wanting to do anything to hinder his recovery. The nurse looked at her kindly and said, "Doctor said try not to wake him. He's still not fully conscious."

"Okay, thank you," Rebbie said as the nurse left the room. Moving closer to Isaiah, she whispered, "Oh Daddy… it just wasn't your time. I love you so much." With tears in her eyes, she gently held one of his hands and rubbed the side of his face.

*****

At home, Angela moved around the kitchen listening to music and putting food on the stove for dinner. "Look like I'll be home alone again. The second *fregado* night, E!" she said out loud in the empty house. "I need to do shit in life, too," she whined. "There's *mierada* I wanna do." As soon as she was done pouting to herself, she heard a loud engine outside. She looked out to see E's car backing into the driveway.

187

"I'll be right back," E told Ben and jumped out, heading to the front door. He walked inside to see Angela coming towards him from the kitchen.

"Hey! Where you been, baby?" she asked.

"Baby, I'm pissed right now, so don't ask no questions."

Angela stood quiet for a few seconds but then yelled out, "Hell no, E! We need to talk! I need to know where we stand!"

"Some East Atlanta dude shot Pop last night!"

"What?! Stop playing," she said, raising an eyebrow like she didn't believe what she was hearing.

"Why would I lie about Pop getting shot?" E asked with a disgusted look. He walked off toward the bedroom with Angela following close behind.

"No, wait! I'm sorry. I didn't mean it that way," she said, trying to explain. "Is he alright?"

E pulled off his shirt and then grabbed a fresh one from a hanger in the closet. He also reached to the back of the closet and pulled out a shotgun. "That bastard hit him twice and *still* didn't kill him. Then J playing that boss man role with me at the wrong time. I will kill that muthafucker like he's a stranger," he snorted with rage. Angela stared in silence as E loaded shells into the gun and went on talking as if his brother was there in front of him. "Don't play me like I don't count for nothing! You ain't having the top spot. Twin brother or not, you got to go!"

Angela made a step toward E and held out her hands to try and

touch him to calm him down. "Listen to yourself," she said softly.
You don't mean that. Brothers should never wanna *kill* each
other."

"When your brother try to steal what's yours- *your inheritance,*
where's the love in that?"

For a second, Angela stood speechless, but moved forward
again when E started to leave the room. "Don't do nothing stupid,
E!" she shouted.

"Get the hell out my way!"

*****

Black woke suddenly from his sleep and sat up in bed. He
looked to one side to see Tina still asleep under the covers.
Grabbing his gun, he looked out of the window and then went to
the bathroom. After splashing his face with cold water, he stood
up and was startled by Tina's reflection behind him in the mirror.
"Girl! You almost got shot, creeping up on me," he said, laughing.

"Everything straight?" she asked.

He turned around, kissed her quickly on the lips and smacked
her butt. "Yeah, we might actually be safe for a day or two. It's
after three and nobody knocked yet."

"I told you when you shot that old guy, he was their main
concern. You showed them you don't give a fuck about blasting
they ass."

"I guess Nicole kept her mouth shut for once."

"She better! Much shit she talk about keeping it real," Tina laughed.

"We got a pickup to make tonight," Black said. "Okay. Let me take a shower and throw on something.

"You do that."

Chapter Sixteen

Rebbie moved between her bedroom and master bath, packing another overnight bag for the hospital. She heard her cell phone ring and answered. It was J. "Mom, where are you? I've been calling you," he said.

"At the house. I got good news," she said, smiling. "The doctor let me see Isaiah, which means he's doing better!"

"Is he awake?"

"No, but he opened his eyes for me," Rebbie said excitedly.

"That's great, Mom. When I get off, I'll be up there."

"Okay," Rebbie said and then asked, "Did you find the guy?"

"Not yet. But I spoke to Uncle Walter," J said, changing the subject.

"You told him what happened?"

"Yeah. He said for you to call him as soon as you can." "I'll call him later," Rebbie said, then looked at her phone. "I got another call coming through. Talk to you later, baby."

"Okay," J said and hung up.

"Hello…"

"Hey Mom, this is Angela. E told me the news. I'm so sorry! How's Pop doing?"

"Thank you, baby. He's better than yesterday. In stable condition – a big change from being in critical last night.

Everybody's praying and staying positive."

"Mom…"

"What, Angela? What's wrong?" Rebbie asked, growing concerned.

"E ain't doing' too good. He was talking crazy just now."

"About what? Talking crazy how?" Rebbie could hear Angela's voice shaking, which made her more and more nervous.

"I never saw E so angry at his brother. The things that were coming out his mouth got me concerned for J's life."

"What did he say?"

"He said that J was just another person and he didn't care about taking his life."

"What?! Is that boy crazy?"

"All I know is, he kept yelling about his inheritance."

Rebbie rubbed her forehead and sat at the foot of her bed. "Lord, the devil is busy."

"I know. It was strange seeing him act that way."

"I'm gonna call him. But if he shows up there, do not argue with him. Just call me," Rebbie said. "Okay, Mom… bye."

Rebbie dialed E's phone and listened to it ring 10 times before the call went to voicemail. Next she called her brother, Walter.

"Rebbie!" Walter answered the phone happily, but then asked, "Is everything okay with Isaiah?"

"Yes, Walter. I saw him yesterday. He coming around. But listen to me… your big sister needs you."

*****

"Tonio, it's me and you," E said. "Ben, just chill out. If you hear my 40 cal pop, you got the Mossberg in the trunk." He placed a hand over his face and swerved his head. "My state of mind ain't tolerating no games tonight."

"Yeah that's how it is, mon," Ben agreed as E and Antonio got out of the car and began walking towards T-Man's door.

"Watch these broads," E said to Antonio. "I can do that with no problem."

Standing to one side, E rang the doorbell and waited. About a minute passed before a pretty latin girl answered the door with one of T-Man's bodyguards standing behind her. "Hi… E, right?" she asked with a smile.

E grinned and nodded yes.

"T-Man is waiting," she said before turning to Antonio, "and I can get your partner a drink." Antonio stared back at her for a second, caught off guard.

"Nah, I'm straight," he finally replied. "I'll just wait here."

The woman walked in front of E, leading him to T-Man's office. She ushered him through the door and then closed it behind him. T-Man stood as E approached his desk, and they shook hands. "Talk to me about the two flunkies."

"Rock robbed me for eighty grand and Black put two shots in somebody dear to me," E said matter-of-factly.

T-Man's expression changed immediately, and he shouted, "Whoa man! Did this person *die*?"

"Nah! But reckless shit was done by both your dogs!"

"Were they together?" T-Man asked, sitting back down in the chair behind his desk.

"Nah… one in Gwinnett and the other in Dekalb," E answered. He stood watching as T-Man leaned forward in his chair and rubbed his fists together.

"Gwinnett… that's your subsistence. Them muthafuckers showed out," he said, shaking his head. "When you take them under your wing and teach them who not to steal from, and who not to kill, it don't stick. They always fall back to that nigga mentality." T-Man picked up a cigar from a dish on the desk and re-lit it. After a couple of puffs, he continued, "I cut Black loose. His loyalty was never there. Turning out some of my bitches on that pill poppin' shit. And Rock… he was just a *do boy*."

"So Rock never put in work for you?" E asked.

T-Man shrugged and shook his head. "He paid to play – a trick. He played messenger on your birthday. That's all he good for. Whatever money he had came from Black. But people like Black won't never cut the pie right. So now…" he flicked ashes from the cigar, "they beefing with each other."

"You was wrong five years ago," E said. "He never was faithful."

"Dishonesty could never stay dormant forever, E."

E laid his palms flat on the desk. Eyeing T-Man, he said, "I need that info. Where they lay their heads."

"Slow down E, and let's rewind. You mentioned someone special. How important is your peeps? In terms of…"

"You taking it there?!" E shouted, cutting T-Man off. He stood up straight and took a step toward the desk that stood between them.

"Business, E. By the time you catch them assholes, your money will be gone. Think about it," T-Man said calmly. "Rock want four keys and he's ready to spend that eighty with me.

Where else he got it from? This his short-lived come up. That's the most cash he's gonna see. Is your peeps worth eighty?"

E watched T-Man through the haze of smoke coming from the cigar that hung between his lips. "Be for real! That's nothing, feel me?"

"Alright then," T-Man said and laid the cigar back onto the desk, "let's say we do this. I give you two of Black's main ho's addresses – one by the name of Tina. And give Rock a time to buy them bricks. I'll make it his *last* drug deal."

E rubbed his chin. "I'm still spending my money though, and I don't trust you to kill that bastard." He nodded toward the closed door behind him. "My brother Tonio will make sure. Just get him where he supposed to be and hit me off with that true address, and it won't be no problem between me and you."

"Good deal," T-Man said with a nod. "Justice has a price, E. Little monkeys is all they are."

*****

Rebbie sped toward the hospital and dialed J's phone. She pulled into the parking lot just as he answered the phone. "Hey baby, everything okay?" she asked.

"Yeah. You at the hospital?"

"Just pulled in. You talked to your brother?" she asked.

"No, not since the hospital."

"Alright, well listen," Rebbie said, "make sure you come by the hospital."

"Mom, you know better than that. I gotta see Pop."

"I know baby, I'm sorry. I just got so much on my mind." Rebbie took a deep breath and looked around at people walking in the parking lot. "Joe caught him yet?"

J looked at his phone, wishing he had some good news for his mother. "I ain't heard nothing. Just be calm, Mom. You know Pop is in good hands."

"Okay, son. Mom loves you."

"Love you, too. See you soon."

*****

The lights were dim in the living room where T-Man sat relaxing on a sofa while the pretty young Latina massaged his shoulders. He gestured for her leave and then picked up his nearby phone to dial Rock. "What's good, young boy?" he said when Rock picked up.

"Waiting on you, big dawg."

"Yeah, I got you them four," T-Man said. "We still talking

196

twenty thousand for each?" "Yeah, I got you locked in for that price." "That's a bet! So, what time we talking?"

Hearing the excitement in Rock's voice, T-Man smirked. "Big Heavy got you," he said. "Just meet him at East Lake Park at eleven. Pop the hood of your car so anybody watching would think you got car problems. Heavy move quick, so be there. Easy transaction, feel me?"

"I'll be there, big dawg... later."

"Peace, young brother," T-Man said and hung up the call. He opened a dark grey case that was at the end of the coffee table, took out four keys of cocaine, and placed them on the table. "Yo, Heavy!" he called, and soon Heavy was standing in front of him looking over the product that was laid out between them. "Here's four birds," T-Man said, staring him in the face. "Make sure you bring that back, plus my eighty-thousand. We talking eleven tonight at East Lake Park. I told him to pop the hood on his car.

That way E man can make a easy spot."

Heavy listened in silence, and then nodded. He placed the packages into a black duffel bag and turned to leave. "I got you. Later."

*****

Rebbie pushed the door to Isaiah's hospital room open and was surprised to see Leah sitting in a chair next to his bed. "Hey, Leah!" she said in a loud whisper. "I didn't know you was here."

"Where you been?" Leah asked her sister.

197

"Coming from home. Packing some things for my Daddy, and making calls," Rebbie said, patting the overnight bag that hung from her shoulder.

Leah smiled. "I figured that. I haven't been here long. They let me see big brother," she said, looking at Isaiah. "I prayed to God for his protection and for Joe to catch the dumb ass that shot him."

"Don't worry, Sis," Reebie said. "God got everything in his hand. Best believe that."

"I know he do," Leah said and reached to grab Isaiah's hand. "I just can't stand to see him like this."

Rebbie walked over to rub Leah's shoulder and then bent over to kiss Isaiah's forehead. "I say the same thing. That's why we gotta be strong."

"Did they catch the asshole yet?"

Rebbie sighed. "Not yet. I asked J, and he said Joe and them was still out looking for him."

"Alright," Leah said with a sympathetic look.

"Sis, I wanna thank you for being here for us," Rebbie said with tears in her eyes.

"When a crisis come, that's what family does. Be there for one another."

Miles away, J sat behind the wheel, driving to the hospital with Rachel in the passenger's seat. They both were in a somber mood, and J had turned the music volume down low so they could barely hear what was playing. Suddenly, Rachel broke the silence between them. "Pop is gonna pull through just fine," she said.

"I know he will. It just pisses me off I can't be out there looking for that fucking coward."

"Don't sweat it, baby. They'll get him soon," Rachel said, grabbing his free hand.

"I hope so, 'cause I'm steady sending up prayers."

"You gotta hold it down," she said. "I know you wish you could be out there putting in work, but they need you at the office right now. Don't let it piss you off. Some dumb ass negro thinks it's all over, but he'll get caught slippin' *watch*!"

*****

Rock looked at his phone again to see the time was 10:45. He and one of his partners, Dino, sat inside a car at the park with the hood up. They both looked around nervously.

"Man… why the fuck we gotta sit here with the hood up?

T-Man be on that stupid shit, my nigga."

"Chill, nigga!" Rock shot back. "That's how he want it done, so his man dropping off would know it's all good. And if anybody being nosey, they would think we got car problems."

Dino rubbed his chin, continuing to look around. "Dawg, this better not be no fucking set up."

"Dawg… we bout to be *kingpins* round this bitch! That muthafucker T-Man, whatever he is… Black or white… is 'bout his paper, folk. He ain't turning down no 80 g's, nigga!"

"I hear you, bruh," Dino said. "What about Coco? Who you

think killed your girl? That's your baby mama, nigga" he said, shaking his head. "Good thing your little girl wasn't there, cuz. Shit… that would've been ugly, folk."

Rock looked out across the park and sucked his teeth. "That cracker E comes to mind first 'cause of who we stuck up. But for real, it could be *any* nigga from the hood looking for a score, 'cause them niggas know I sell them killa pounds." Thinking about Coco, he shook his head. "I can't sweat that shit now. Coco knew what type of life we live, my nigga. She was my baby mama and all, but all women like her can be replaced."

"I feel you," Dino said. "But if it was that cracker, his 80 g's is about to be spent."

Rock threw his head back and laughed, "Damn right, cuz! Every cent!"

On the other side of the park, Antonio and Mackie stood outside their vehicle. "Mackie, look in the back seat and pass me them night owls," Antonio said.

"Time to pull out the high-tech shit on these niggas," Mackie said, handing over the binoculars.

"Damn right, bro. E put me onto this muthafucker. A good soldier stay on point." Antonio adjusted the binoculars and peered across the park. "Yeah… that's what I'm saying! Night vision. Got that pussy all lit up, bro!" He had a clear view of Rock and Dino and watched as Dino got out of the car without a gun and stood in front of the vehicle.

Dino folded his arms impatiently and looked around him. "This muthafucker need to hurry his ass up! *Shit*!"

"Chill out, nigga! It's all good. We sitting on eleven o'clock," Rock shouted from inside the car.

Just then, Dino saw headlights coming down the street and tapped the side of the car to get Rock's attention. "Yo Rock! I think this is that nigga coming now." Rock got out of the car with a gun at his waist and stood at the front of the car beside Dino. They watched as a car rolled slowly towards them.

From across the park, Antonio saw the car driving toward Rock and his companion. "Yo, there he go pulling up now. You go around and come up from the back, and I'm gonna walk straight to 'em," he told Mackie.

"Bet! Do your thing – I got you."

Rock and Dino didn't move until the car came to a stop just a few feet away, and Heavy got out carrying a large black duffel bag. Seeing the bag, Rock smiled and took several steps forward. "What's good, big dawg? You got that?" he said, nodding toward the bag. He reached and took the bag as Heavy handed it over. Looking inside, Rock's smile grew even wider. "Shit… look good, my nigga!" None of them saw Antonio creeping up.

"What's up, bro? Y'all got car problems? I'm a mechanic."

Surprised, Rock jerked around to see Antonio. "Hell nah, Jose! Nobody called you. Get the fuck outta here!"

"You know my man, right?" Antonio asked. "Nah, nigga! I

don't know *your man*."

"Yes, you do! White Boy E told me to give you this."

Antonio quickly pulled out a gun and pointed it at Rock. Heavy stepped to one side while Dino slowly moved towards the passenger door of the car.

"Fuck, my nigga! We got set the fuck up!" Dino yelled.

Figuring Antonio was distracted, Rock tried to grab a gun from under his shirt. But Antonio delivered two shots – *Pop! Pop!* - and Rock fell to the ground. Dino made it around to the side of the car and opened the door just as Mackie came up behind him and pointed his gun at the back of his head. "Too slow, nigga. Turn around. I like looking a nigga in his eyes before I lay his ass to rest."

"Nigga, fuck you!" Dino screamed.

"What, muthafucker?! Fuck this!" *Pop!* A shot was delivered right into Dino's face, and his body slumped and fell into the car. Mackie lowered his gun and flexed his shoulders, turning his head back and forth. "I feel good now," he said calmly.

"Go collect your money, big dog." He watched Heavy open the black bag and get the money out of Rock's car. "Let's bounce, bro."

*****

J stood beside Isaiah's hospital bed, watching his father's chest move up and down. The monitors, iv, and oxygen were still connected, and Isaiah had not regained consciousness. Rebbie sat

202

in a chair beside the bed watching J. Suddenly she stood and moved toward the door. "Sit here and talk to your daddy," she told J. "I'll be in the waiting room."

"All right, Mom." As soon as Rebbie walked out into the hallway, J leaned close to Isaiah's face. "Can you hear me? It's J," he said. To his surprise, Isaiah's eyelids fluttered. Then his eyes opened, and began to speak softly.

"Hey, son."

J's eyes filled with tears and he leaned even closer to his father. "Pop, I been praying like you taught me." He was happy to see his father's faint smile. "I love you, Pop. I'm staying strong and keeping the family together like you'd want me to."

"Where's E?" Isaiah asked, looking past J and around the room.

"He'll be up to see you. Everybody staying strong for you. I'm doing what you taught me. Don't worry about nothing, Pop. I'm keeping the family together." J felt Isaiah give his hand a hard squeeze before closing his eyes again to rest.

Chapter Seventeen

E and Ben sat in the car, waiting in silence. Suddenly E's phone rang. He answered it and put the call on speaker. "We good?"

"He's a done deal, bro. Him and his little shooter," Antonio said on the other end.

"Caught 'em together, huh? Two down, one more sucker to go. Alright… I'll get wit'cha." E hung up the phone.

"Wah gwaan? They kelt de bumbaclot?" Ben asked. E nodded. "They did their thing. T-Man's halfway true so far."

"Them ras-clot wanna be gangstas!" Ben crunked up the car and started to drive.

E sat in the passenger seat, staring ahead and mumbling to himself, "Fuckin J, you muthafucker… I'm putting a stop to you. Killing souls tonight, no matter who!" Then, looking out of the window he told Ben, "Hit this corner store. I got a taste for something sweet."

"Me need full up 'on sum Guinness and Black & Mild, mon," Ben said, pulling into the parking lot.

"I got you, bruh." E shook his head. "I don't see how you smoke that shit."

"Me need me smokes, mon!" Ben said laughing.

Inside the store, a young woman leaned on the front counter and yelled to a couple at the back. "You niggas need to hurry up! I'm trying to smoke something!" Coming through the door, E looked at the female and then walked past her and turned down an aisle where he saw Black and Tina. Caught off guard, E hesitated for a moment. He locked eyes with Black, who gave him a puzzled look.

"Oh shit, you look familiar, man! Hold on…" he said, pointing a finger at E, "… hold on. I know you."

"What's up, Black?" E said.

"Your name E, right?"

"Yeah, that's me, dawg."

"Yeah… from *way* back," Black said with a chuckle. He turned to the woman who was with him and said, "Hey Tina, this white boy cool as fuck." Turning back to E, he asked, "Shit, what you up to, boy? You see what I got. I'm 'bout to go smoke one. You still don't smoke?"

E shrugged. "I smoke a lil something."

"Muthafucker all grown up now," Black said, raising his chin, eyeing E from head to toe.

"Gotta be that good shit though, feel me?"

"Ah man, this ain't none of that shit we gave that young boy that night," Black said. "That pussy ass nigga had to go."

"I hear you, man. I got my partner in the car. That's cool?"

"Shit yeah. Bring that nigga. I got *this* fine young thing right here, too," he said, slapping the girl on her behind. Nodding in her direction, he said, "He can have some. Shit! Nigga ain't stingy when it come to pussy."

"Damn, girl, sexy! What's your name?" E asked the female.

"Lexi," she answered.

E smiled and winked at her. "I like that. Sexy name for a sexy woman." Looking back to Black, he said, "I'll follow you to the spot, man."

"Do that," Black answered. "I'll be out in a minute."

Back in the car, Ben looked confused when E got inside. "Where me Guinness?"

"Fuck a Guinness! We got three bodies to kill," E answered.

"Who dat?" Ben looked around outside the car.

E held up his hand to silence Ben. "Watch," he said, staring at the front of the store. A few seconds later, Black and the two females walked outside. E pointed at Black. "It's Mister Black and his two bitches."

"What boi! Guinness can wait, mon. Bumbaclot!" Ben pounded the steering wheel with his fist. Looking at E, he said, "God brought them right to ya, mon."

"Divine shit. We got that invitation, dawg. Got that sucker fooled. Made him think we come in peace… then we blast everybody."

"Oh zeen, mon!" Ben said, rubbing his hands together.

E pulled out a flier showing a picture of Black. "When I toss this flier in his hand, you know what's coming next," he said.

"Shoot em up, bang-bang! Him and his bitches, ya know!"

*****

In the hospital cafeteria, Rebbie and J stood holding hands, and

206

with their heads bowed in silent prayer. Rebbie had asked J to come down to grab a quick lunch, but there was more on her mind. "Amen," she said softly and squeezed his hands. Then, "I need you to listen to me. This is important."

"What is it?" J sensed the concern in her voice. "Your life, baby."

"What you mean?" J shrugged and shook his head.

"Your brother…" Rebbie hesitated, "… he done flipped out. E got the devil in him. He talking about killing you." She reached into her purse and pulled out a sheet of paper. J stared at the paper and was shocked to see it was the old agreement he and E had both signed when they were kids. Rebbie continued, "I found this. I don't wanna know why y'all did this. But I know he don't wanna honor what he agreed to. So, I'm asking… no, I'm *telling* you to go to Uncle Walter's until he calm down. 'Cause if he kill you, I'll kill him."

J looked puzzled. "My brother wanna *kill* me?"

"That's the mind state he is in right now. And I gotta keep that from happening. The devil is not gonna win this one. We done came too far," Rebbie said, grabbing J's hands again.

"I can't just run like some punk," J said with anger rising in his voice. "You and Pop always taught me to stand firm."

"Shut up and listen, son! This ain't nothing about being a punk. You have to always pick your battles wisely. I got a lot to deal with right now. Isaiah laying up in there all shot up," Rebbie said, nodding toward the wing outside of the cafeteria, "and I need to focus on him getting better with no evil in my midst." She looked up at her son and searched his eyes. "This is the only way, J. Please listen to your mother. I'll handle E when I see him." She could see that J was reluctant and felt him trying to pull away. But she held on to him tightly.

*****

The smell of cigarette ashes filled the air inside the interrogation room. It was humid and dark, except for the tabletop right beneath a single bulb hanging from the ceiling. Kenya sat on one end of the table, leaning into the light and staring at Nicole, who was handcuffed and sitting in a metal chair. A male detective stood in the dark against a wall.

Nicole sat with her back straight, staring straight ahead. "I told y'all I have no fucking clue on their whereabouts!"

"Girl, use your damn brain!" Kenya shot back. "Black could give less than a damn about you! He got Tina now. If he cared anything about you, your ass wouldn't be here."

The other detective walked from the shadows and approached the table. "You better think hard about it. You're looking at an attempted murder charge, *plus* aiding and abetting a fugitive. Is that scum worth 10 to 15 years?"

"So… what's in it for me?" Their words were beginning to sink in. Nicole squirmed in her seat and began to bite at the loose skin on her bottom lip.

208

"A lesser charge," the male detective answered.

Nicole looked over at Kenya, who nodded in agreement. "That ain't telling me shit!" she yelled.

"Maybe getting it reduced to a simple obstruction charge," he said.

"A whole lot less than attempted murder," Kenya chimed in.

Nicole leaned her head to one side and stared at the wall. "I ain't no snitch."

"Nobody said you were," Kenya said. I'm just asking you to do the right thing. We need to get Black off the streets. We need your help, Nicole." Kenya watched as the young woman slumped in the chair and dropped her head, and then raised it again to look at both her and the other detective.

"I need this shit in writing."

"Not a problem. I can guarantee it," the male detective said.

Finally, Nicole closed her eyes and took a deep breath. "Tina stay on Camp Creek Parkway at some apartments called Creekside Grand."

"I need the whole address," Kenya said. "We can't be running up in the wrong apartment."

Nicole rolled her eyes and slumped even lower in her chair. "Building 5, apartment 5-2-1." Kenya and the other detective exchanged looks before both leaving the room.

******

E and Ben followed Black and the two girls to an apartment

and then followed them inside. The front room was lit by only one small lamp with a dark shade. The musky smell of incense was heavy in the air. "Y'all gone ahead and get comfortable," Black said and pointed to one of two couches that crowded the small room. One of the girls, Lexi, followed Ben and sat on his lap with one arm around his shoulders. E sat down at the opposite end of the couch and kept an eye on everyone and everything happening around him. He saw the girl Tina walk down a hallway to a back room, while Black sat on the couch across from him and opened up a stash box that sat on the coffee table. Seconds later, he was rolling a blunt, but stopped to press a button on the remote that was also on the table. Reggae boomed from the speakers on the sound system.

E recognized the song and started to bob his head. "Turn that shit up, man! That shit tight! Who dat?"

"My man, Damian Marley! Distant relation. That shit drop last month, mon." Ben held up one arm and grooved to the music from his seat. "Yeah mon, shit hot!"

"What's the name of that track?" E asked.

"Patience," Black said. "I listen to that shit when I smoke. Keep a nigga in chill mode, boy."

E nodded his head. "That's what I be telling this young rap dude – *be patient*, you gonna get your turn to shine."

"Who this nigga, dawg? Somebody local?" Black asked.

E lifted his lower body from the couch and pulled a folded

piece of paper from his back pocket. "Shit, I got his flier right here. He reppin East Atlanta."

"Word! I probably know that nigga. Let me check that shit out." Black reached to grab the sheet of paper and studied it for a couple of seconds before his expression changed. "What the fuck, man! What the fuck is this?!"

"Don't act like you don't know what the fuck you did!" E yelled.

"Fuck you saying?" Black had a look of deep questioning on his face.

"That was my dad you shot! Bitch ass!" E pulled the gun from his waistband. When Black reached for his, Ben pushed Lexi from his lap and stood up from the couch.

"Get off me, yeh stinking bitch," he sneered and then shot her the second she hit the floor.

"Now… smoke *this* muthafucker!" E said, pointing the gun at Black. He shot him twice in the head and watched him fall back onto the couch. Down the hall, a door slammed shut, and Ben rushed toward the back of the apartment. He kicked in the door, and E could hear Tina screaming.

"No, please! No! No!"

"Ya bumba ras clot!" Ben raised his gun and delivered two shots to Tina's chest. Before her body hit the floor, he turned and was walking back into the front room.

E stood near Black's body and grabbed the flier that was still on the couch next to him. "Let's get the fuck outta here!" he yelled over the loud music that was still playing.

Chapter Eighteen

Rachel sat on the edge of J's bed, watching him pack clothes into a small duffel bag. Her overnight bag was beside her feet on the floor, but she hadn't packed anything. Silently, she watched J move back to the closet and return with a gun, which he put into his bag. "Why all of a sudden?" she finally asked.

"What are you saying?" J asked, shifting things around in the bag.

"What made you wanna get a room tonight? Don't you think Mom needs us?"

"Mom already know. Everything is cool," he said. "She thought it might be good for us. I spoke to Annette, and she invited us to the talent show at the Hyatt Regency." J stopped and looked up at Rachel. "I know things are the way they are, but we still gotta live our lives."

"I know, J. I'm just concerned about Mom and Pop."

J shook his head and smiled. "Mom ain't your average woman. Once she puts her request in to God, it's a wrap!"

"I know that first-hand. Mom's that role model type. I see some of her in you."

"Oh yeah? Like what?"

"Compassion and love for the truth of all things," Rachel said, putting her hand on top of his.

"Right now, the truth is you need to hurry up packing 'cause I'm ready to get you in that king-size bed, Miss Rachel the opera singer!"

"Ah… yes, yes! Ah, yes, baby!" They laughed and hugged each other. Minutes later, they walked out of the bedroom and then left the house for the night.

*****

"You pissed off the wrong shooter, home boy." Joe stood in the middle of the room looking back and forth between the two bodies on the scene, one of which was Black, shot dead and slouched over on the couch. The other body belonged to Lexi, lying on the floor across the room. Both bodies lay in massive amounts of nearly dried blood. Joe looked at Kenya, who was walking carefully around the scene and shaking her head.

"We got one more dead body," another officer said, walking from the back of the apartment. "Looks like our other suspect, Miss Tina."

"So that makes three," Kenya said, coming to stand beside Joe. "Mr. Samuels won't be living that thug life no more."

"Whoever it was made damn sure of that," Joe said. "They shot him close range. Two shots to the head was all it took. Well, at least Rebbie gets to have some closure."

*****

Ben pulled his car into E's driveway and sat with the engine idling. He and E looked at each other, and both shook their heads with a sigh. "Task completed, bruh," E said. "We did good. Caught them bitches off point."

"No talk from dead ones, ya know. What 'bout J, mon?" Ben asked.

"I'm the only one that throw out questions 'bout my brother, feel me?" E said with a hard stare.

"Yeh mon. Every'ting kris."

E's expression softened suddenly, and he reached to slap five with Ben. "Go get some rest. And tell Tonio to lay low today. We got a few dead bodies scattered all over."

"Me ah watch some tv and close me eyes, boi," was Ben's reply.

"Do that," E said, opening the door and stepping out of the car. He watched Ben back into the street and drive away, then walked slowly up the driveway and got into his own vehicle.

*****

Rebbie stood at the stove in her kitchen, enjoying the early morning quiet of the house. She put a pot on the stove, and then reached for her cup of coffee on the counter. Suddenly, her phone rang and she answered. Hello?"

"Hello. Good morning, Mrs. Jones. This is Carlos."

"Hey, good morning!"

"Good morning, ma'am. Just wanna let you know the guy who shot Isaiah was found dead this morning."

"Really?!" Rebbie covered her mouth with one hand and began bouncing on her toes. "Who killed him?"

"That's not clear right now, but he got what he deserved.

Everybody can sleep a little better now…" Carlos paused. "Where's the twins?"

Rebbie was smiling and waving her hand excitedly in the empty kitchen. Looking around her, she shrugged and said, "J's not here, and I guess E is at home. But I'll tell 'em both the good news!"

"Yeah, I'm pretty sure they would wanna know."

"Amen to that!" Rebbie said and hung up the phone.

Miles away, in a hotel close to Midtown, J sat in the bathroom in his and Rachel's room. She was asleep in bed, and he talked in a low voice to his uncle Walter on the phone.

"Hey, J! Where you at, man?" Walter asked. "Rebbie told me your flight was at seven-thirty, coming from Atlanta."

"Mom told you right," J answered. "Listen Unc…" J paused, "… it was last minute. I had to make some changes. We straight… everything is fine. But I never made that flight. I'm still in Atlanta." Before his uncle could respond, J told him, "Mom think I made that flight… and that's the way I need it to stay."

*****

"Come sit down in the den," Rebbie said, leading Kenya from the side door and through the kitchen. They hugged and then sat on the sofa. "Glad you came over," Rebbie said with a smile. But then, seeing the troubled expression on Kenya's face, she asked, "What's wrong?"

Kenya shook her head and said, "Rebbie, E is extorting a store owner. Why, I don't know, but it don't look good."

"Extorting?!" Rebbie leaned away from Kenya. "Extorting what, Kenya?"

"Looks like it's for money. When I saw him, my mind was blown!"

"Money?" Rebbie stood up from the couch. "Has that boy lost his damn mind?!" She started to pace the room. "Isaiah wouldn't believe the foolishness his son is into. Behaving like a damn criminal!" Turning to look at Kenya, she said, "He is following in the same footsteps as that young boy who shot Isaiah. Now, whoever it was who killed him did us a damn favor. The wicked shall not go unpunished!"

*****

Isaiah's hospital room was empty, except for E standing directly over him beside the bed. Tears welled up in his eyes as he watched his father's motionless body. "Hey, Pop. Open your eyes," he said. "Hey, tough guy. It's E... can you hear me?" He reached out a hand to lay it on Isaiah's shoulder, but stopped himself. And suddenly, Isaiah's lids fluttered, and his eyes were open. He looked directly at E and smiled. Excited, E smiled back. "What's up, Pop? How you feel? I got some chocolates for you."

Isaiah held out a hand and began to speak slowly. "Okay... that's good. You made time for your Pop?" He smiled again and when E grabbed his hand, he squeezed it tight.

"I love you, Pop. I was just being stupid and self-centered and

217

wasn't thinking about the family. Big mistake. This wasn't supposed to happen to you." He looked away and shook his head. "My brother took what you offered to me. He running things. What do I have to do to regain your approval?"

"What's done is done," Isaiah answered in a low scratchy tone.

"Don't lose faith in me. I can do it, Pop. I'm ready to step in."

Isaiah frowned and shook his head. "Love J and support him."

Disappointed at his father's answer, E lowered his head. "I been there for J, in all truth, since we were young boys. Have faith in me," E said, looking back into his father's eyes.

"I do," Isaiah answered. "You doing good. You got family, money… *women,*" he said, managing a smile. "I can't give you something that God already did. Heaven is here for you." Isaiah closed his eyes and began to draw deep, heavy breaths.

"Pop! I'm the oldest. I'm your strength and you know that!"

A young nurse walked into the room, and E let go of Isaiah's hand. "Your father went back to sleep on you?" she asked with a laugh.

"You can say that. It didn't take him long, either. That medicine be doing the job!"

"Don't feel bad. He did your mother the same way yesterday." The nurse checked numbers on the bedside machines and then wrote notes on her chart. Before leaving the room, she stopped to try and fluff the pillows beneath Isaiah's head.

E leaned over and kissed his father's forehead. "I hear you,

Pop. But do you hear me?”

*****

J walked out of a convenience store and towards his car in the parking lot. He was finishing a conversation with Joe on his phone. “Man, that’s a big relief! I ‘preciate that, Uncle Joe!” He got into the car and sat staring at Rachel for a second, taking deep breaths. “We got him!” he finally yelled.

“Really?! Yes!” She pumped her fists with excitement. “Baby see, I told you he wasn’t getting away with it.” Looking at the phone in J’s hand, she asked, “What did he say?”

“The guy got gunned down on the West side. He was found murdered early this morning.”

“Uh-huh! God don’t like ugly… so that’s what he get! If I’m wrong, please forgive me, Lord…” she said, looking up and holding her hands palms together, “… but I don’t think so!” She looked back at J. Did you speak to Mom yet?”

“Nah, Uncle Joe just called me.” “What about E? Do he know?”

“He probably found out before me,” J said with a smirk, staring off into the distance. “But anyway,” he said, looking at Rachel, “Ain’t no need to talk to Mom if she calls. This is our time, feel me?”

“Okay… but what if she need to reach one of us about Pop?”

J placed his hand firmly on the console between them. “Don’t answer the phone, Rachel! Is something wrong with me wanting

219

no interruptions? Damn! Pop is fine. I'll check on him later…
okay?"

"Whatever you say, baby. I'm sorry." Rachel leaned over and
gave him a kiss.

*****

Anna, Antonio's cousin, sat watching the evening news and
coverage of two dead bodies found in East Lake Park. "What you
know about that?" she asked Antonio.

"You sound fucking crazy, fool!" He was instantly defensive
and raised his voice. "Don't put me with that *mierda*!"

"Ha!" she said, sucking her teeth. "Nigga, I may be crazy, but
I ain't *loco!* I know who you work for."

"We cousins and all, but you better watch that word play
'round here… singing out the side of your neck." He leaned toward
her with two fingers pointed like the barrel of a gun. "Shit ain't
sano for you!" he said with a cold stare.

Anna shrugged and held up both hands. "I'm just saying,
Tonio."

"Don't make me repeat myself, *prima*. Don't do it!

*****

E wheeled his car through Isaiah and Rebbie's neighborhood
with one hand while holding the phone to talk to Honey with the
other. He pulled into his parent's driveway and cut off the engine.
"No doubt, sexy. I'll be stopping by later."

"*Muah*!"

220

"I'll be waiting," Honey replied with a kissing sound.

"Damn girl! I like them kisses for sure. Later, sexy." He hung up the phone and then hopped out of the car and headed for the front door. Unlocking the door with his key, he walked inside where, as soon as she saw him, Rebbie came at him in a rush.

Pointing a finger in anger, she said, "What's this I hear 'bout you wanting to kill your brother? Are you out of your damn mind?!"

"What? What are you saying, Mom?" E was startled and took a step back.

"Where the hell were you on February 23rd, 2005, which was on a Sabbath?"

E looked at his mother, still confused and speechless. Rebbie held a wrinkled piece of paper in front of his face. It took a few seconds for E to read the first lines and realize what she was holding. "Where do you get this?" he asked.

"Don't you worry," she said with an angry scowl. "I see you signed over what Isaiah had for you. Now you wanna kill your brother! Whatever the hell you was doing, I don't wanna know. But if *that* goes down… I'm coming after you." Rebbie planted both her feet as if to square off with E. "I brought you in, and I'll take your ass *out*," she warned. "Now try me if you like.

You might scare them dummies out there in the street. But that nonsense ain't moving nothing over here!"

E took another step back and held out his hands. "Cool out,

Mom! Don't come at me like this."

"Cool out hell! I mean what I say!"

E suddenly stopped backing up and raised his voice to his mother. "J trying to keep me out the business! I asked him who it was that shot Pop, and he didn't wanna tell me! He's letting things go to his head! That ain't how you treat family, and you know it. I got a right to know who shot Pop."

"You better lower your voice in this house before I knock your head off," Rebbie said, pointing her finger and stepping into his face. "You might raise your voice at them dingbat women you mess around with. But I'm your mother and don't you *ever* forget it!" She lowered her finger and her voice and backed up. "Nobody said you didn't have a right to know who shot your father." She looked at E and rolled her eyes. "You wasn't interested before… remember? I see it takes an accident for you to show your father attention. That's not honor. It's more like dishonor."

Her words stung and hit home. "You know Pop wanted me to take over, not J. I'm the oldest."

"Boy, you got the devil in you. Making threats to people in the street?" Seeing his dumbfounded expression, Rebbie nodded her head. "Think Mom don't know! What's done in the dark always come to the light. You ain't ready to run no business. I won't have you destroy something your father built."

"What? Where is this coming from? I can run the business with no problem! And who was I supposed to be intimidating? I keep it peaceful wherever I go!"

Rebbie walked away, shaking her head and laughing. "Your mother knows." She then turned to him and said, "You look at me and lie! If you lie, you steal. Behaving like you had no home training. What you do in them streets comes back on your father and me. You and your brother represent us and the Father every time you step foot out that front door!" She walked away again and sat in Isaiah's favorite chair. "Uncle Joe found the guy who shot your father. Young guy just like you… dead! And if your ass don't straighten up, you gonna be next. God gave you one brother to love… not kill! You better tell Satan to stand back."

"Oh really?" E said in a dismissive tone. "I hear you. Where's J?"

"I'm not telling you nothing til you get your head straight."

"I ain't trying to hear this madness… pulling stuff out the sky!" E walked from the room and out of the house. Rebbie got up from the chair and followed him outside.

"Call it what you want, son. The Father knows. You better take heed, E!" she called from the porch, watching him get into his car.

"Whatever, Mom."

Rebbie clasped her hands together and looked to the sky. "Father," she said softly, "only you know. I'm prepared for whatever you decide."

Inside the car, E turned his music up loud and looked over his shoulder to back out of the driveway. Then without looking back at his mother, he hit the gas and sped off down the street.

A short while later, he was at Honey's house lying across her bed. She had set a nice, relaxing scene with the lights dimmed and soft music playing in her bedroom. Walking from the bathroom, she slid onto the bed beside him and ran her hand along the side of his body. "You never talk much about your family," she said softly.

"What's the need to? Why should I?"

"I *am* fucking you," Honey said, sliding closer to him. "Maybe I would like to know more about you besides your penis size."

E shrugged and said, "I'm a twin. He doing his thing. I'm doing mine."

"Damn, that's crazy! You got a twin?" Honey said, sitting up on the bed. "There's two of y'all running around Atlanta? Damn, what I'm fucking with?" She laughed and laid back onto the pillow.

"You gotta put it like that?"

"Not in a bad way, baby. I mean… twins have that special connection… that bond. If one hurt, the other one feels his pain," she said, looking E in his eyes. "Twins run in my family. I think it's cool. Shit… I wish I was a twin."

"It's just you?" E asked, suddenly interested to know more about her.

"Just me," she sighed. "It was boring being the only child. Not having nobody to play with. I suffered, but made it through. The older I got, friends came and went. Well, who I thought were my friends anyway. A bunch of liars is all they were."

"That's all some folks do is bullshit, like they get a check every week for being fake."

"Cherish that shit though, for real," Honey said, patting his arm lightly with her fist. "A twin brother…" her voice trailed off. "If anybody would be there, I bet he would." She stared at him for a few seconds and then said, "You know what?"

"What's up?"

"I'm glad we met."

"Me too, baby."

"So anyway… like I was saying earlier, I got a surprise for you. I hope you like it," she said smiling. "It may be different from your spot. A little less fighting and muthafuckers losing their money. Just a little change baby, that's all. I know it will leave a positive effect on you." She leaned forward and kissed him on the lips.

*****

E held his hand lightly at Honey's back as they walked along the aisle to find the row with their seats. When they arrived, the lights in the auditorium were already low, but they could still see the faces of people sitting near them. E looked around and recognized some entertainers. Soon, a young performer came on stage and began to sing.

"Alright now! Girl, sing that song… sing it!" Honey shouted. She was on the edge of her seat, enjoying the performance. E smiled, realizing he was on an actual date with his jump-off.

225

J and Rachel looked out into the hotel from inside the glass elevator as it glided down toward the lobby. He smiled and looked at Rachel from head to toe. "Damn! You looking *and* smelling good!"

"You too, handsome! I hope we didn't miss Annette's performance."

"We should be good," J said, looking at his watch. "They just started."

"Ooh… baby, I'm excited!"

The elevator chimed and the doors opened when they reached the ground floor. J grabbed Rachel's hand as they walked off together.

*****

There was thunderous applause inside the auditorium as the young singer took a bow and then left the stage. The emcee for the night returned to the spotlight and spoke to the audience. "Let's give it up for Miss Gloria Brown!" E and Honey and the rest of the crowd continued to clap and cheer. "Man! That sista can *blow*! Matter of fact, she can sing to me *every night*!" the host said, causing the crowd to laugh. "But coming to the stage next is a very talented, outspoken sista from Decatur where it's greater! She's going to be giving us some spoken word." He turned and waved an arm toward the side of the stage. "Give it up for Miss Annette Williams!"

Annette walked onto the stage while the audience clapped. As soon as E saw the young woman, he sat forward and said, "Yo! I know that female. Damn, I know her!" At the same time, J and Rachel walked into the dark auditorium and found their seats.

They were on the opposite from E and Honey. Just as they sat down, the applause quietened, and Annette began to speak.

Withdrawn from the man is a true fact! Woman kind, delicate, compassionate once upon a time. It's our turn, 2010 a new trend in the Earth. We have surpassed our man, Black woman.

Statistics are high! Single moms, Section 8, incarceration awaits our young. Illiteracy surrounds me. Neglecting our babies is what I mainly see. 4-year, 6-year degrees – college-educated, independent and proud. Ignorant of your identity.

Black is a color, not your nationality. Having a position to play is what we were born to do.

Never forgetting our foremothers who fought, prayed and died for our rights America once denied.

Now you call yourself a diva. Foul-tongue Jezebel with a stretched neck and wanton eyes. Blood pressure rise, redness succumb my eyes. Angry? Damn right!

Ho tatts above the ass crack. Back in the day, sistas knew better than that. Polluting the land, switching from man to man…

Both E and Honey, and J and Rachel sat listening silently, intrigued by Annette's verses.

Assuming he's gonna keep it true because he penetrated you. HIV, syphilis - catch me if you can. Fair play, trick or treat some say. Bringing forth monsters to oppress and slay their own.

Woe to you! My womb is God's crib, you feel me?

Precious to him. No foul creatures shall step in. Laws made clear from the start. Put your weed down! Ease up on the drink and think!

Virtuous, never flirtatious. Older women do you damn job. Teach the young women how to love a man. Keep your feet not in the street, but in the home which are tender.

Remember your purpose, Black man. Provide! Protect! and Teach is the task. Stop the witchcraft, dope sales, genocide. Not much longer will Christ sit back and watch his people die.

Pants sagging, boasting, keeping up drama every day. You party without a conscience. Rulership is what you should claim. F- the fame! Put away the PlayStation game.

Shit is vital out here. Young boys roam the street packing heat with evil eyes toward their elders. No more good rap, just gun clap.

We learn from what you do. The man being the head. With that being said, who's the blame? Listen up! Wake up! The end times. Last days.

UFOs patrol the skies. Disciplined angels on standby – wheels of fire!

Professional liars have become the person to be. Society built on lies, many lives sacrificed

For the evil cycle. God's law taught the opposite way for personal gain. Sex wolves feeding his flock confusion in the brain, lusting with no regard. Perverts in every hood.

You come not in peace, but division. Big hats, tight see-through dresses first lady prize possessions every Sunday. It's all fashion.

The Father always chooses the lesser. My favorite Biblical sista, Esther never forgot her people, her kinsmen, siblings a tight fit.

Close-knit family is special to see. Love! Respect! Brother to brother remain united between each other. Brought forth with a purpose. Childhood, school days. Times you could never get back. Cherishable years, moments to hold dear…

Listening to Annette, E began to think about fun times in the past with his brother. He pulled out his phone and sent a text to J: What up, bruh? We need to talk.

Annette continued onstage:

Differences shouldn't resort to death but understanding. A world in which truth must be placed on high. Kill the uproar before too much pain is unable to contain…

J received the message from E and texted back: Hit me up. When E saw it, he tapped Honey on her arm. "I'll be right back," he said and got up to leave the auditorium.

Spirits trapped inside, they cry aloud! Death is near! Above the clouds birds fly. Faith is all it takes. Perfection is what I pursue and so should you. Foolishness must perish from among us.

Judgment covers all. Awareness is priority.

Exercise loyalty - humanity is at risk. I pray you all paid attention to this!

Thank you very much! Atlanta, I love you!

As the crowd erupted into applause, J's phone rang. Covering one ear, he answered it. "Hello? Hello!" The call disconnected and he looked at the phone. "I'll be right back, baby. That was E calling."

"Ok, baby," she said, barely paying attention. "My girl threw down! She told the truth!"

While Annette was at the mic bowing to the applause, the emcee walked back onstage. "Give it up for Miss Annette Williams!

Sista broke it down!"

J walked up the main aisle and out into the lobby. His phone rang again and he answered, "Hello, E! What's up?"

"What's good with you? Check this out," E said. At that moment, he looked up and saw J standing at the other end of the lobby. He could tell that J saw him as well. He hung up the phone and started walking toward his brother. "J!"

"Damn boy! I guess it wasn't meant for us to talk on the phone," J teased. They both laughed and reached to give one another a hug.

"That's your friend onstage speaking, right?" E asked. "Yeah, my girl Annette. She tight, right?"

E sighed and shook his head. "Man, she was speaking the truth, putting muthafuckers in check! Had my mind flipping back."

"No question. She make peeps take a look at themselves.

I had a feeling your ass was out here," J said, grinning at E.

"I felt the same thing. He rather us settle things in person," E said, lifting his eyes toward the ceiling.

J nodded in agreement. "That's the best way. The eyes don't lie." He looked E in the eyes and said, "I feel that your spirit is at ease."

"I feel good. The message came at the right time. I wanna let you know some things are meant, lil bruh. You stepped up not for yourself, but for the whole family. Sticking to an agreement has to be honored, feel me?"

"We get off track sometime. If life is lost, then unnecessary pressure creeps in. We smarter than that. Pops didn't shoot out no dummies."

"That hate crept in, lil bruh. Shit tried to have me break our commitment. You didn't hesitate this time, I did. You stepped up and put work in for Mom and Pop," E said.

"I should'a told you from the jump who shot Pop," J said.

"I understand. You held back for the right reason.

Loyalty is important, right? Shit falls apart without it. We shared the same womb. I came out white and you Black. That has great fucking significance! Being that light for the world has to be the mission. No bullshit."

"No doubt. We gotta play our spot at a high level. That's the law." J grabbed E to pull him close for another hug. "Love you, bruh."

"Love you, lil bruh… remember that."

Suddenly, they heard applause from inside the auditorium and remembered there was still a show going on inside.

"Who you out here with?" J asked.

E grinned and said, "I got my brown Honey with me."

"What?! A sista? Who is she?" J asked, and they both laughed. "Aha! Look at you switching up!" They walked back toward the auditorium doors with arms over each other's shoulders.

Reviews

"E & J is a gritty urban saga reminiscent of the tale of Cain and Abel. The author takes you on a journey from the unusual circumstances surrounding the birth of twins E and J, through trails that test the strength of their family and bond as brothers, to realizing that love and family are their sustaining force. Author Michael Williams, also provides engaging visual references to help draw the reader into the character and situations contained in his work." 4.5 stars - Sherron Nesmith of Sparrow Communications

"E & J is a best seller, significantly different, nothing comes close in this day and age. The story flows well, characters are believable and many of them have strong roles. Art work portrays truth that the reader can identify in today's society. E & J is a must read!" 5 stars - Gary Tavares C.E.O of Tavares ENT.

"Raw emotions, realistic character struggles and biblical knowledge included in this book. Literary masterpiece!"- 5 stars – Reader.